CU00664252

CONTENT

INTRODUCTION

Caring for your inner child has a powerful and surprisingly quick result: Do it, and the child heals. – Martha Beck

Childhood is often represented in poetry and fiction as a beautiful, magical experience. While this is the case for some, it isn't so for everyone—childhood, alongside old age, is one of the most vulnerable stages in the human life cycle.

Who you are today depends on the myriad of experiences, thoughts, emotions, and beliefs you first encountered as a child. It results from deeply entrenched family patterns, values, and ways of viewing the world and interacting with others.

If you have experienced trauma, neglect, abuse, and other behaviors and attitudes that affected your core beliefs, values, and self-esteem, it undoubtedly affects who you are today.

A study of 17,000 adults showed that 66 percent of them had experienced at least one adverse childhood experience (ACE).

What's more, one in six had experienced four or more ACEs. These experiences include[1]:

- experiencing physical or emotional abuse
- witnessing a parent being abused
- being abandoned or neglected
- losing a family member
- growing up in a household with substance abuse or alcoholism
- having a mentally ill parent
- having an imprisoned parent
- being a child of divorced or separated parent

There are various risk factors for experiencing ACEs, including coming from a low-income family or one with a low level of education, growing up with high levels of family stress, being raised among family members who do not communicate their feelings openly, and having parents who use physical punishment.

When your inner child is hurt by trauma, it directly impacts your thoughts, emotions, and behaviors. Let's take an example from everyday life. Imagine you are in your office, and you ask your colleague a question. If your colleague doesn't give you the time and attention you seek, a barrage of thoughts may take over your mind. You may think, *They think they're better than me; They're so unprofessional;* or *They're users and only friendly when they want something from me.*

In this case, you may not have all the evidence needed to make these assumptions that are as harmful to others as they

---

1 Wisner, 2022.

are to yourself. It's easy to see that if you accept that these negative automatic thoughts are true, your relationship with your coworkers can be harmed. You could end up avoiding chances to collaborate with them on work projects or interact socially. In the end, others could form close bonds, leaving you behind.

When you have a hurt inner child, it isn't easy to control these automatic thoughts. Left to run amok, they can lead to emotions such as sadness, disappointment, and resentment.

In the example of the dismissive colleague, perhaps you reacted so vehemently because your inner child has always felt belittled or undervalued. You may have grown up in a home where your parents worked so many hours they weren't able to give you quality time. Perhaps you grew up with adults steeped in high levels of stress who did not react as patiently and calmly as you needed.

When your inner child is wounded, you try to defend it vehemently because the adults in your life have not loved, protected, or defended you as they should have. However, hurt inner children often choose the wrong coping mechanisms, resulting in impaired goals and relationships.

In the above example, a useful coping strategy might be to wait until your colleague is less busy, write them a follow-up email, or even suggest a drink or coffee outside work one day so that you can bring up your concerns.

An unhelpful coping strategy, on the other hand, includes avoiding them in the future, being rude to them when they ask you for help, or criticizing your colleague to other people instead of dealing with them directly.

Working on your inner child through cognitive-behavioral therapy (CBT) techniques will help you reap many rewards. First, you will learn to quickly identify negative thought patterns and stop them in their tracks before they affect your emotions. Moreover, you will hone key strategies to reframe these thoughts, so you can take an evidence-based approach to what is going on around you. In essence, you will work on transforming yourself from a reactive person to a proactive one.

My goal in this book is to help you recognize and heal your inner child. In Part I, we will begin by journeying to the past and discovering why your inner child may be hurting. We will get straight into CBT activities from the start, providing you with activities that will help you meet your inner child for the first time.

We will then analyze how your inner childhood experiences influence your attachment style. The relationships you build in childhood have a powerful influence on your social, intimate, and professional relationships. If you have attachment trauma, it is vital to know the signs and embrace scientifically proven strategies for changing your attachment style from insecure to secure.

In Part II, we will begin the first of five steps to heal your inner child. We will discuss CBT—including its core principles and strategies. In the following chapters, we will employ specific

CBT strategies to reframe your thoughts, emotions, and behaviors.

Building emotional intelligence is also vital if your inner child is in pain. Emotional intelligence enables you to perceive, evaluate, manage, and express your emotions to achieve your goals and build healthy relationships.

Once you are familiar with CBT and you have completed various exercises, you will benefit significantly from knowing your inner child's specific triggers. You will discover how to combat these "enemies," many of which you may have been battling unsuccessfully since early childhood.

Finally, in the bonus chapter, you will discover two additional approaches to boost inner child healing: neuro-linguistic programming (NLP) and acceptance and commitment therapy. They take very different approaches to the process of healing. Still, both are focused on helping you see things in a more positive light, enhancing your self-awareness, and building and maintaining healthy relationships.

As a child, you may have viewed the adults around you as sources of stress instead of love and care. As such, you may mistrust others and find it hard to establish meaningful bonds, take part in collaborative ventures and activities, and celebrate the joyous wonder of maintaining a childlike outlook regardless of your age.

There is an adult that will stand by your side unconditionally if you let them. That person is yourself—the guardian and protector of your inner child. Before you start this book, take a photo of yourself when you were young and post it somewhere you can see it often. When you're about to say negative things to yourself or be less kind to yourself than you would to someone you love, take a look at that picture. Whatever you choose to give yourself—be it anger, fear, sadness, compassion, or kindness—you are giving to that child. Let's work on giving them the love and care they deserve.

PART I

1

WHO IS YOUR INNER CHILD?

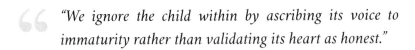

"We ignore the child within by ascribing its voice to immaturity rather than validating its heart as honest."

— CRAIG D. LOUNSBROUGH

THE IMPACT OF TRAUMA

Trauma has a big impact on children who experience it, and the hurt it causes is carried on into adulthood. Those who have experienced abuse, neglect, and other adverse experiences can have issues such as low self-esteem, anxiety, and depression. Some deny their traumatic experiences and history, while others create a false self-image and engage in alcohol and drug misuse in attempts to escape from the impact of trauma. Trauma doesn't just go away. Its effects last in the long term if you don't intervene and employ tried-and-tested strategies to deal with it[2].

2 Downey & Crummy, 2022.

EMMA

Emma grew up in a relatively stable family that didn't function as healthily as it could. Emma's parents were in a co-dependent relationship. Her father, Kenneth, had a bad temper and poor anger management skills, and he was very strict with Emma and her older sister Mara. He often raised his voice at his daughters, who were always scared to say or do something that displeased him.

Emma and Mara's mother, Sarah, was relatively kind to her daughters but was very much centered on Kenneth. He had various narcissistic traits, and Emma recalls that Sarah enabled them and behaved like his full-time cheerleader. Sarah's goal was to bolster her husband's ego, take his side whenever he got angry at someone, and get just as angry at her daughters whenever her husband raised his voice at them.

Kenneth often accused his daughters of doing things they hadn't done; he refused to let them interact freely with other kids their age and often snapped without provocation. Sarah never corrected his bad behavior toward his daughters but was over-critical of Emma and Mara, who never seemed to be "good enough" in her eyes.

What was most painful for Emma was that when Kenneth would say something out of line, her mother would say that Emma had provoked the situation. She would also turn the story around and gaslight her daughters, giving a version of events far from the truth.

Mara and Emma adopted very different coping strategies. Mara put on a confident facade but would radically cut off anyone from her life whose behavior reminded her of her mother's. Emma, meanwhile, continued to be a people pleaser, failing to set boundaries, overworking, and trying hard not to disappoint anyone. It led to stress, burnout, and, eventually, isolation. She just couldn't keep giving herself to others when she was running on empty.

Both Mara and Emma had hurt inner children. Mara's bravado enabled her to set boundaries, but these were often too rigid. Anyone that threatened them was eliminated mercilessly. Emma, meanwhile, had greater difficulty both in her social life and at work. She took negative feedback as a personal slight, obsessed over the tiniest mistake, and, deep down, felt unworthy. Both could have used inner child healing to be happy within themselves and embark on healthy relationships—those in which communication, feedback, and a commitment to hearing and seeing others are prioritized.

WHY YOUR INNER CHILD MATTERS

Acknowledging, addressing, and taking time to heal your inner child is important because doing so enables you to address needs that have not been met as children. It also allows you to be kinder to yourself and prioritize self-care[3].

----

3 Trieu, 2023.

A BRIEF HISTORY OF INNER CHILD THEORY

Inner child theory can be traced back to Carl Jung, who made a powerful discovery after looking into his own childlike emotions. He proposed that we all housed an inner child who influenced our decisions and actions. Our inner child absorbs all the experiences, thoughts, and emotions we have—good or bad. They are formed when we are completely dependent on our caregivers. Unfortunately, our inner child does not forget the criticism, betrayal, or hurt they encounter. Once our inner child experiences trauma, it can resurface in our adulthood, negatively influencing our relationships and decisions[4].

WHEN IS YOUR INNER CHILD FORMED?

There is no specific age during which your inner child is formed. Rather, the inner child is a synthesis of all ages and continues to form as you transition into old age. Each developmental age represents one small part of who we are. Assagioli (1973) stated that the union of all these ages could be achieved by "keeping the best aspect of each age alive.[5]"

WHAT ARE THE SIGNS THAT YOU HAVE A HURT INNER CHILD?

When your inner child is wounded, you may feel specific emotions or display characteristic behaviors. You may[6]:

- feel broken
- be scared of being abandoned

---

4 Davis, 2020.
5 Assagioli, 1973.
6 Rediscovering Sacredness, n.d.

- tend to say sorry when you have done nothing wrong
- feel chronically angry, resentful, or frustrated
- have high levels of anxiety
- have obsessive-compulsive tendencies
- find it hard to say no
- have difficulties with boundary-setting
- give more to others than you reasonably can
- close yourself off from others
- dissociate ("leave your body" during stressful events to avoid pain)
- mask trauma through poor eating habits
- try to go unnoticed through how you dress, the colors you wear, etc.
- become obsessive or fixated on details in an attempt to attain perfection
- become obsessed with your physical appearance
- take too many risks
- be an overachiever

As Mara and Emma's story shows, some people are more efficient at hiding their hurt from others and themselves. They may decide to protect themselves at all costs, inadvertently hurting others with their rigid standards.

THE SEVEN INNER CHILD ARCHETYPES

In her book, *How to Do the Work*, Dr. Nicole LePera defines seven inner child archetypes[7]. Knowing these archetypes can be of vital importance when you work to re-parent yourself and acknowledge your deficits or wounds.

---
7 LePera, 2021.

The seven inner child archetypes are:

1. **The Caretaker:** This inner child can arise after exposure to codependent dynamics. They gain their sense of identity and self-worth by neglecting their own needs. They believe that to receive love, they need to sacrifice themselves for others.
2. **The Overachiever:** This inner child only feels seen, heard, and valued when achieving things.
3. **The Underachiever:** This inner child doesn't try to succeed because they fear criticism or failure. As such, they quit the emotional game before it's ever played.
4. **The Rescuer/Protector:** They try to be someone else's hero or to protect or rescue them from pain. They believe the only way to receive love is by helping others solve their problems. Oddly enough, rescuers derive their self-worth from being in a position of power.
5. **The Life of the Party:** This inner child feels like they must always be "up" and happy. They may have been shamed in the past for showing their emotions, so they get used to hiding them.
6. **The Yes-Person:** They have trouble saying no. They are similar to the caretaker in that they derive value from always being available to others and ceding to their demands.
7. **The Hero-Worshipper:** They need a person or guru to follow. They may have perceived a caretaker as flawless and perfect. They believe that they have to deny their own wants and needs to follow the lead set by their hero.

All these archetypes display unmet emotional needs and a lack of connection. Their behaviors are conditioned by familial patterns and repeated exposure to specific behaviors. These patterns are converted into narratives that determine how we see life and interact with people around us.

Many of your personality traits are learned behaviors from your early childhood. However, accepting these traits as "who you are" can be detrimental. This is why it is important to acknowledge and name the things that have broken you. If you simply let things continue as they are, your hurt inner child will continue to scream for attention[8].

THE BENEFITS OF HEALING YOUR INNER CHILD

To meet, acknowledge, and re-parent your hurt inner child, you must be committed and set time aside to discover more about yourself and engage in CBT activities. You will find that this is one of the most worthwhile investments you can make in your health, happiness, and well-being. Just a few of the many benefits of healing your inner child include[9]:

- an enhanced understanding of your pain
- the ability to discover your boundaries
- moving toward wholeness
- discovering how to identify narcissistic abuse
- learning to set boundaries

----
8 Wisteria Edwards, 2021.
9 Gatt, n.d.

THE BEAUTY OF THE INNER CHILD

Inner child work is not exclusively centered on the trauma you may carry from childhood. It also involves allowing your inner child to "come out and play." You know your happy inner child is there when you are[10]:

- losing yourself in an activity you love
- laughing with your friends
- playing with games, toys, or pets
- feeling emotional when you view old videos or photographs of yourself as a child
- still thinking or behaving as a child in the very best sense—being playful, gentle, and cheeky.

Acknowledging your inner child enables you to prioritize doing the things that you love and excel at. These activities are an essential means through which to exercise self-care.

MASLOW'S HIERARCHY OF NEEDS

Your inner child can be hurt if their basic needs are not met. At this stage, discussing Maslow's Hierarchy of Needs is helpful. Developed by American psychologist Abraham Maslow, this theory suggests that people have a set of basic needs that must be fulfilled before they can move up the hierarchy to pursue more social, emotional, and self-actualization needs[11]. This does not mean one need must be satisfied 100 percent before the next need emerges. Instead, when a "deficit need" (an unsatisfied need) is more or less met, it goes away, and we focus on

---

10 Health Vista, n.d.
11 Cherry, 2023.

meeting the next set of needs we must satisfy. The ultimate goal is self-actualization—which effectively means that you are realizing your full potential.

Maslow's Hierarchy of Needs is as follows[12]:

1. **Physiological Needs:** These are our basic human survival needs—food, clothing, and shelter. All other needs become secondary until these needs are satisfied.
2. **Safety Needs:** These include protection from the elements, the law, stability, and freedom from fear.
3. **Love and Belonging Needs:** The third level of human needs focuses on the feeling of belonging and having healthy interpersonal relationships. Examples of love and belonging needs include friendship, intimacy, trust, giving and receiving affection, and acceptance.
4. **Esteem Needs:** These are divided into two categories: 1. esteem for oneself (comprising achievement, mastery, independence, and dignity) and 2. the desire for respect or reputation from others (comprising status and prestige). Maslow stated that the second category is the most vital for children and adolescents and precedes the need for self-esteem and dignity.
5. **Cognitive Needs:** These include curiosity, exploration, gaining knowledge, and the search for meaning and predictability.
6. **Aesthetic Needs:** Human beings naturally seek out beauty, balance, and form.
7. **Self-Actualization Needs:** These include seeking personal growth and peak experiences, realizing your

---

12 McLeod, 2018.

full potential, finding self-fulfillment, and (as Maslow stated) the desire to "become everything you are capable of becoming."

Transcendence Needs: Motivation can be found in things beyond the personal. They include mystical experiences, interactions with nature, sexual experiences, the sense of fulfillment from serving others, the pursuit of faith and/or science, etc.

Questions to Ask Yourself: The hierarchy of needs is vital to know and analyze when working on your inner child. Try to think of each rung in the ladder of needs, and ask yourself: Were any of these needs unmet during your childhood and adolescence? How does this impact your relationships, goals, decisions, and actions? Which of your needs do you feel was most neglected?

WHAT DOES BEING SELF-ACTUALIZED FEEL LIKE?

Maslow stipulated that when you heal your inner child and reach a state of self-actualization, you develop specific characteristics. They include:

1. viewing reality efficiently and having a good tolerance for uncertainty
2. accepting yourself just as you are
3. being spontaneous in thoughts and actions
4. knowing how to focus on problems (instead of being self-centered)
5. having an unusual sense of humor

6. being able to see things objectively
7. being creative
8. being resistant to the gradual acquisition of the characteristics and norms of a culture or group without being purposely unconventional
9. sharing concern for others' welfare
10. having the ability to deeply appreciate the basic life experience
11. establishing deep, satisfying relationships with a few people
12. enjoying peak experiences
13. needing privacy
14. embracing group decision-making having democratic attitudes
15. having strong ethical or moral standards

HOW CAN YOU REACH A STAGE OF SELF-ACTUALIZATION?

In order to feel like you are living your best life, the following strategies can help[13]:

- Experience life like a child, with full concentration and absorption.
- Try to accept things as they come, adapting to changes instead of being angry that they have changed your plans.
- Live spontaneously, without analyzing every action and plan too much.

---

13 Raypole, 2020.

- Enjoy a little "me time" and see it as a way to reconnect with yourself.
- Be grateful for the little things in life—including affection from a pet, a good laugh with a friend, and a nice meal.
- Be true to yourself and others, avoiding lies, manipulation, and denial of your needs.
- Hone your compassion. Be a good listener, give yourself fully to others when you are with them and make them feel heard, and try to find ways to give back without expecting anything in return.
- Seek therapy if you need extra help to identify your goals and embrace the strategies you need to get there.

3 ACTIVITIES TO MEET YOUR INNER CHILD

If you have unmet needs, or you are showing signs of housing an inner child archetype within you, then it is time to introduce yourself to your inner child for the first time. Below are three activities catered to this purpose:

Guided Imagery Exercise

Picture yourself resting on the seaside at sunset. There is a little child who approaches you from the other side of the cove you are sitting in. When they are close enough to hear you, you approach them, take them in your arms, and ask them to tell you what is wrong. You tell them, "You deserve to be loved. I want to give you unconditional love, even though I did not have this kind of love when I was a child."

Tell your inner child, "Change is positive. I will work to heal you, but I won't forget you, even when I feel strong and happy.

"I am talking to others to receive support; I will tell them our story. My friends (or therapist) are important to me because they can help you and me heal."

"You help me believe that recovery is worthwhile. To help heal you and heal me, I will make healthier decisions and stop feeling guilty about the past. I will value you and me, and stop feeling bad when I have to say no to others or set boundaries to protect us."

"If we keep behaving the way we always have, things will never change. I want to be with you and honor you in the best possible way by ensuring we are safe and secure and that our boundaries are respected."

"By working to heal ourselves, you and I can unite and do the things we love—like eating our favorite food, playing the games we love, and laughing with abandon."

"I know that by being kinder to myself, you will be happier because you love me as much as I love you. You see abilities in me that I don't know I have, and you help me believe that life can be better."

"To let go of our trauma, I have to let go of self-pity, anger, and shame. That might be very difficult, but it can help if I start treating you the way I would have liked to be treated."

"By working to strengthen my body, mind, and spirit, I will also make you stronger."

"Let's celebrate our new journey and look forward to the moment when we are united in health and happiness."

Now, you can allow your inner child to leave. They will always be with you, and you can call them back to your side to celebrate your achievements on your journey toward healing.

Inviting Your Inner Child to Play

Tap into the fun side of being a child and allow your inner child to play in a safe setting. Just a few ways you can connect with them include:

- Do something messy—like baking, growing a vegetable garden, or sculpting.
- Treat yourself to something you would have liked as a child. This item could be a stuffed toy for your desk, a shoe with a little sparkle, or a clothing item in your favorite color when you were a child.
- Have a forest bath. Head to a green area—preferably the woods—and take part in *shinrin yoku*—a Japanese practice that involves opening all your senses to the beauty of nature. Listen to the rustling of leaves in the wind and of little insects playing in the scrub; look around you, taking notice of the height, width, and color of the plants and trees. Touch items with different textures—including leaves, flowers, roots, and tree bark. Smell the plants and flowers around you. Bite into a fruit and enjoy its delicious sweetness.

- Speak up and tell the simple truth the next time someone asks you for your opinion.
- Spend time with children and play with the games you used to enjoy as a child.
- Do something purposely destructive such as punching a beanbag, shredding used paper, or throwing a plastic toy to the floor.

The next time you are worried or tense, conjure up your inner child and talk to them. Let them know you will look out for them and that there is no need to be afraid.

A Journaling Exercise

Throughout this book, I will suggest using a journal to record your thoughts and emotions. Write down the following questions and answer them[14]:

1. Were your parents physically and emotionally present during your childhood?
2. Did you feel like your parents loved you exactly as you are? Or did you feel that you had to prove your love, make certain achievements, or display certain behaviors for them to accept you?
3. Did your parents encourage you to set boundaries and limits? Did they allow you to say no and speak your mind, or did they punish or reject you when you spoke your mind or were honest and assertive?

---
14 Williams, 2022.

✎...

✎...

✎...

✎...

Now that you know who your hurt inner child is and you are ready to take the steps you need toward healing, it's time to discover how they are affecting your relationships with others.

2

HOW YOUR CHILDHOOD EXPERIENCES INFLUENCE YOUR ATTACHMENT STYLE

"It is the experience of loving and being loved that most closely predicts how we react to the hardships of life; human attachments are the ultimate source of resilience."

— JONAH LEHRER

ATTACHMENT THEORY: THE PAST INFLUENCES THE PRESENT

Renowned British psychoanalyst John Bowlby espoused that your relationship with your parents during childhood has an overreaching influence on your social, intimate, and work relationships[15]. His theory suggests that from birth, human beings need to forge close bonds with their caregivers. The bonds they form (or fail to) have a major impact on subse-quent life attachments.

---

15 Cherry, 2023.

Human infants crave closeness because it is essential for their survival during the process of evolution. In order to forge vital bonds, infants and toddlers monitor their parents in order to discover the strategies that allow them to stay close[16].

When parents or caregivers are available and responsive to an infant's needs, they enable the child to feel secure. The infant learns that their parents or carers are trustworthy and dependable. This creates a secure base from which the child can then explore the world.

SAM

Sam grew up in a home where forgiveness had to be begged for, and respect was demanded rather than earned. His mother, Grace, had very exacting standards when it came to communicating assertively (without raising one's voice or displaying uncontrolled anger).

The problem was that Grace took little of her own advice, often speaking at a loud volume and sometimes using physical force to make her children snap out of a tantrum or moment of upset. When she did blow up, Grace punished Sam by forcing him to sit in a chair for a couple of hours without allowing him to read or distract himself. For the next day or two, she would completely withdraw from her son, who used to have to write her letters and beg for forgiveness before she finally acceded. Most of the time, Sam apologized profusely, not because he thought he was wrong, but to once again be in his mother's "good books."

16 Mandriota, 2021.

This behavior hurt Sam's self-esteem. When he grew older, he continued to try to people-please but tended to get into relationships with non-committed partners. He was unable to spot or process the signs that others were toying with him and believed they loved him as he loved them. It took many years and heartbreaks for him to realize that he could not go on hurting himself that way. He had to learn that, like many of his good friends, he deserved to be in a loving, nurturing relationship. Inner child work helped him connect with the abused child he used to be and begin the process of healing. In his late 30s, he met a partner who was committed to him and vice-versa. To this day, he works hard to exercise self-care and self-compassion.

THE FOUR STAGES OF ATTACHMENT

Researchers Rudolph Schaffer and Peggy Emerson performed a study involving 60 infants. They observed them every month during their first year of life and then again at 18 months. Based on their observations, they discovered four different phases of attachment[17]:

The Pre-Attachment Stage: Infants aged zero to three months do not demonstrate any particular attachment to their caregivers. When they cry or fuss, they are attended to by their caregivers, and their positive responses promote closeness.

Indiscriminate Attachment: Between six weeks and seven months, infants start to show a preference for their primary caregivers. By now, they trust that their caregiver will fulfill

----
17 Edward, 2017.

their needs. They accept care from other people but seek out their primary caregiver more than they do other people.

Discriminate Attachment: Infants demonstrate a specific preference and strong attachment to one person from around seven months of age. They may cry when they are separated from this person and feel more anxious than in the past when approached by strangers.

Multiple Attachments: From around 10 or eleven months of age, babies start to form strong attachments to other caregivers in addition to their primary caregiver. For instance, they may start seeking out their other parent, siblings, grandparents, aunts, and close family friends.

THE FOUR ATTACHMENT STYLES

There are four main attachment styles:

Secure

When you have a secure attachment style, you can do the following.

1. Regulate your emotions.
2. Trust others easily.
3. Communicate your wants and needs effectively.
4. Seek emotional support.
5. Enjoy being alone.
6. Feel comfortable in close relationships.
7. Manage conflicts productively.

8. Enjoy a healthy sense of self-esteem.
9. Be emotionally available when others need you.
10. Trust your partners so that jealousy and intentions are not causes for concern in your relationships.

Avoidant (Dismissive or Anxious-Avoidant in Children)

When you have an avoidant attachment style, you may do the following.

1. Avoid emotional or physical intimacy.
2. Feel fiercely independent.
3. Feel uncomfortable about sharing your emotions.
4. Dismiss others.
5. Find it hard to trust others.
6. Feel threatened when someone tries to get close to you.
7. Want to spend more time alone than in the company of others.
8. Believe you can do things independently.
9. Have difficulty committing to others in relationships.

Anxious (Worried or Anxious-Ambivalent in Children)

When you have an anxious attachment style, you may do the following.

1. Have low self-esteem.
2. Feel unworthy of love.
3. Fear abandonment.
4. Need approval from others.

5. Show signs of jealousy.
6. Have an intense fear of rejection.
7. Find it hard to trust others.
8. Find it hard to be alone.

Disorganized (fearful-avoidant in children)

When you have a disorganized attachment style, you may do the following.

1. Fear rejection.
2. Find it hard to regulate your emotions.
3. Have high levels of anxiety.
4. Find it hard to trust others.
5. Waver between avoidant and anxious attachment styles.

Secure attachment styles arise when children's needs have been consistently met during infancy. If the bond with parents or caregivers is strained or non-existent, on the other hand, they can develop an avoidant, anxious, or disorganized attachment style. These insecure styles are inextricably linked to the hurt your inner child feels, even in adulthood.

WHAT IS ATTACHMENT TRAUMA?

Relationship trauma expert, Heather Monroe, describes attachment trauma as "a consistent disruption of physical and emotional safety in the family system. It is not what happens to you but what happens inside you.[18]"

---

18 Ryder, 2022.

Attachment trauma can be felt physically as your body enters "fight or flight" mode. The stress you feel can be constant and cumulative. This type of trauma is linked to a disoriented-disorganized attachment pattern that increases your risk of abuse and neglect. It is also closely related to poor overall mental health.

Parents and caregivers who cause attachment or relational trauma often do so unintentionally. In almost all cases, their behavior results from their own untreated attachment trauma. In this way, this painful cycle can continue through generations. By working to heal your inner child, you can break this cycle and empower your children to adopt a secure attachment style.

PHYSICAL OR EMOTIONAL ABANDONMENT?

Sometimes, abandonment is physical. This can occur, for instance, when parents divorce or one or both parents die, and they are no longer physically present to bond with their child[19].

Abandonment can also be emotional. This occurs when a caregiver cannot or does not fulfill a child's need for love, care, boundaries, and other nurturing needs.

Emotional abandonment can arise for many reasons, including:

- a parent or caregiver feeling overwhelmed by parenting and other duties
- too many responsibilities for a parent—including work and relationships outside the family

---

19 Newport Academy, 2017.

- substance abuse

TWO OFFICIALLY RECOGNIZED ATTACHMENT DISORDERS

There are two main types of attachment disorder, according to *The Diagnostic and Statistical Manual of Mental Disorders:*

Reactive Attachment Disorder

Children with this type of disorder may:

- have low levels of social interaction
- show little emotion during reactions
- find it hard to calm down when they are triggered
- seem unhappy, irritable, or sad when engaging in everyday activities with their parent or caregiver.

Disinhibited Social Engagement Disorder

Symptoms of this disorder include:

- hyperactivity
- poor social boundaries or extreme sociability and a readiness to engage with strangers.
- Asking inappropriate questions, and generally showing a lack of inhibition.

Both disorders can arise from maltreatment or neglect.

HOW YOUR ATTACHMENT STYLE AFFECTS PARENTING

We have mentioned that your attachment style can affect your relationships. In cases of insecure attachment styles, for instance, you may be uncertain or jealous, lack self-esteem, or have trouble sharing your emotions. Your hurt inner child may stop you from committing fully or trusting your partner and other important people in your life.

When your inner child has unhealed wounds, it can also influence your parenting style[20]. In other words, as long as you are still hurting, it can stop you from being the most nurturing parent to your own children.

Parenting With a Secure Attachment Style

If you have a secure attachment style, you can be close to your child while still seeing them as a separate individual. You meet their needs for love and care, empathize with how they are feeling, and try to be fully present for them.

Parenting With an Anxious or Preoccupied Attachment Style

If your parenting style is anxious or preoccupied, you may only be available intermittently. Your lack of consistency can confuse or frustrate your child, who may feel that their needs are not always met. Parents who favor an anxious parenting style may look to their child to fulfill their needs or display an emotional neediness that drains the child's energy and serves as

----
20 Firestone, n.d.

a poor substitute for authentic love and nurturing. Children of parents with this style may become clingy in their own relationships, or they may be insecure because their parents have been inconsistent.

Parenting With an Avoidant or Dismissive Style

Parents with this attachment style may meet a child's basic needs (such as the need for food and shelter), but they may be emotionally unavailable. Children can respond by behaving as though they do not have these needs. They learn to remove themselves from their emotions and tell themselves they are the only person they need to survive. They feel they must avoid expressing their needs and wants and maintain a "safe" emotional distance from others to survive. As adults, they may struggle to form intimate relationships and may accuse their partners of being too needy.

Parenting With a Disorganized Attachment Style

This type of attachment style can arise when a parent is a source of fear for their child. Parents who adopt this style are often inconsistent, thus causing insecurity and fear in their children. For instance, they may laugh at a behavior one day, then explode with anger when their child displays the same behavior another day. The child doesn't know where they stand, and it can feel like they are walking on eggshells. They are afraid to approach their parent, and they feel unsafe. They may love their parent but feel terrified of them at the same time. They may adopt a blend of avoidant and anxious attachment styles in their adulthood. Likewise, they may feel over-whelmed when someone wants to get close to them yet pursue people who are emotionally unavailable.

When embarking on the journey to heal your inner child, it is important to think about the attachment style or styles you grew up with. Analyze how they may have affected the type of relationships you seek out and how you behave during tense moments and conflicts.

The good news is that even if you have an insecure attachment style, you can change it. First, you must face some of your childhood's most painful experiences. Throughout the process, it is vital to be on the side of your inner child; to remember that your main role is to protect them, not to add to their fear, anger, and pain. When you become aware of how your hurt is sabotaging your current relationships, you can take steps to feel more secure, confident, and loving. You can start to trust others and allow them to get close to you.

STRATEGIES FOR CHANGING YOUR ATTACHMENT STYLE

In order to change your attachment style, it is vital to do the following.

Know if your style is secure or insecure. Use the information above to discover whether your attachment style is secure or insecure. If your attachment style is insecure, you may have a blend of avoidant, anxious, and disorganized styles.

Learn from others. Don't be afraid to talk about your inner child. Find out how others have overcome challenges. You may be surprised to discover that some people you see as secure and confident actually had to overcome difficult or traumatic childhoods. Try to observe people with secure attachment styles. What behaviors and words do they utilize? How do they react in times of stress and anxiety? How do they handle conflicts?

Be reflective and proactive. Take specific steps to become more secure. Start journaling, sign up for a mindfulness class, embrace physical activity, harness the power of positive affirmations, and complete cognitive-behavioral worksheets. This way, you can correct negative behaviors that impede healthy connections.

Keep a journal of your emotions. Journaling is a powerful means through which to see how your thoughts, emotions, and behaviors are connected. It enables you to have a record that is valuable both in the moment you write down your emotions and experiences as well as many days, weeks, months, or even years later. It is easy to forget how you once felt, how you dealt with a stressful situation, or how you used to perceive specific situations and people. A journal can help you connect the past and present and reveal important information about your attachment style.

Record the evidence. When you encounter a negative thought or emotion, try to list the evidence for that thought or emotion immediately. This will help you identify when bias and distortion have made you see things in a more negative light than was warranted.

Pause instead of reacting immediately. The old adage of "counting to ten" before reacting to a trigger holds true when it comes to building healthy relationships with others. An insecure attachment style can cause you to think of the worst of others or to attach intentions to their thoughts or behaviors that do not exist. By taking a step back, breathing, and coming back to a problem when you are calmer, you can be assertive instead of reactive and focus on solving a problem instead of on "winning."

Think of the other person. Take advantage of a quiet moment and think about how you would feel if someone spoke or behaved toward you the way you have to a partner, friend, colleague, or family member. It isn't easy to be objective and distance yourself from your own perspective, but if you want to get along with others, it pays to do so regularly.

Analyze your choices. Think about how you chose to respond to a challenge or problem. Was it the most fruitful way to deal with it, or could you have tried alternative strategies? If you find the latter true, don't beat yourself up about not getting it right the first time. Embrace the growth mindset, which stipulates that failure is a magnificent opportunity for growth and positive change.

Express yourself clearly. When you assert your wants and needs, do so assertively and honestly. Try to be spontaneous and to say what's in your heart. Don't worry about being too honest or vulnerable. In healthy relationships, these traits strengthen rather than threaten your bond.

3 ACTIVITIES TO KNOW MORE ABOUT YOUR ATTACHMENT STYLE

If you want to know your precise attachment style, the following websites provide dynamic online quizzes that ask you a series of questions and then provide you with your preferred style. Meanwhile, the activities below will get you thinking about how secure or insecure you are in relationships.

Online Quizzes are available on:

www.idrlabs.com

www.attachment.personaldevelopmentschool.com

www.attachmentproject.com

Questions About Your Significant Relationships and Experiences

The following questions are taken from an adult attachment interview protocol therapists use with their clients. These questions can help you identify secure or insecure behaviors and shed light on your attachment style[21].

- Go back to your earliest memories and write a description of your relationship with your parents.
- What phrases or adjectives come to mind when you think of these relationships?
- Which parent did you feel closest to? Why do you think this was the case?
- When you were upset, what would you do? Who would you turn to?

---

21 Sutton, 2022.

- Can you describe the first time you were separated from your parents?
- Did you ever feel rejected, abandoned, or lonely as a child?
- Did your parents ever threaten you?
- How do you think your childhood experiences affected the way you are today?

Why do you think your parents behaved the way they did?

✎…

✎…

✎…

✎…

Accepting Yourself, Just the Way You Are

If your parents tried to live vicariously through you, expected too much from you, or made you feel like you weren't good enough, your self-esteem may have been damaged, and your inner child may feel hurt and vulnerable. This exercise can help you love yourself with all your perfect imperfections[22].

- In your relationship, when do you expect yourself to be perfect?
- When do you expect your partner to be perfect?
- How do you feel when you do not manage to be perfect?

----
22 Sutton, n.d.

- How do you feel when your partner doesn't manage to be perfect?
- What do you do when you feel this way? (For instance, you might shout, blame your partner, distance yourself from them, etc.)
- What can you say to yourself to show more kindness and compassion to yourself when you fail to be perfect?

What can you say to your partner when they fail to be perfect?

✎...

✎...

✎...

✎...

Tracing Your Insecure Attachment Pattern

In order to understand how insecure attachment impacts your relationships, it is vital to face uncomfortable experiences and analyze how you respond to them. You can do so by taking the following steps[23]:

- Think of an experience in your relationship that made you angry, sad, or uncomfortable. What happened to trigger these emotions?
- Experiences hurt people for different reasons. When you think about the experience above, what was the most painful part for you?

----
23 Callisto Media Books, n.d.

- Think back to your first two decades of life. At what age did you first encounter the experience or emotions mentioned above? Now think about all the other ages you met this experience or emotions again. Include experiences you've had at home, school, work, and social settings.
- Ask yourself if you have encountered these experiences or emotions in one setting more than others.
- Ask yourself who or what made you feel better during these times.

How can you soothe your inner child when you encounter these experiences and emotions today?

✎...

✎...

✎...

✎...

THE POWER OF AFFIRMATIONS

When you are in the midst of a triggering experience, reassure yourself with positive affirmations such as:

- "Don't worry; I accept you just as you are."
- "Your emotions are valid."
- "Stop, slow down, breathe."
- "This experience and these emotions do not define you."

- "You feel this way now, but you probably won't feel the same in a few days."
- "You can find a productive way to deal with this experience. You can use this strategy every time it pops up in your life."

You have immersed yourself in different attachment styles, and you now understand how your particular style can affect the way you parent your own children. It's now time to immerse yourself in a host of CBT-based activities. Part II will focus on CBT strategies to heal and strengthen your inner child.

PART II

CBT STRATEGIES AND EXERCISES TO HEAL
YOUR INNER CHILD

3

WHAT IS CBT AND HOW CAN IT HELP YOU HEAL YOUR INNER CHILD?

> *"In a nutshell, the CBT approach works by identifying, evaluating, and finding new ways to respond to automatic thought patterns."*

— ANNA NAPAWAN

If you have always taken an interest in psychology or you (or someone you love) have anxiety or depression, you may have come across the term *cognitive-behavioral therapy* (CBT).

CBT is considered a gold-standard treatment for many mental issues, including anxiety and depression. Many experts believe it is the most effective treatment for these common mental conditions since it has a 50-75 percent success rate for those who undergo between five and fifteen sessions[24].

If you have symptoms of anxiety or depression that are interfering with your daily life or if they are persistent and long-

---

24 Pun, 2019.

lasting, then it is imperative to seek professional help. Many people also find it beneficial to check in regularly with their inner child by completing worksheets that help them reframe how they think, feel, and behave.

LENA

Lena came from a country that was in the midst of what seemed to be an endless war. Food and basic commodities were lacking, and the sounds of bombing and guns were an everyday occurrence. Lena's parents had to move their family from home to home several times, relying on odd jobs to put enough food on the table. When Lena was two, a terrible massacre took the lives of Lena's parents, and she was placed into an orphanage because her remaining family was unable to take care. Eventually, she was placed in the care of a foster family, but she never managed to form the secure attachments that children need in order to feel happy and secure. As an adult, she battled depression and PTSD, and she also struggled with negative self-esteem[25]. She began receiving CBT as a means to overcome her mental anguish. She also learned to identify the automatic negative thoughts that would pop up in her mind. By analyzing the evidence for those thoughts, she could reframe them and see life through a more positive lens.

----

25 Hasanović et al., 2006.

WHAT IS CBT?

CBT is easy to understand by taking a look at this basic model:

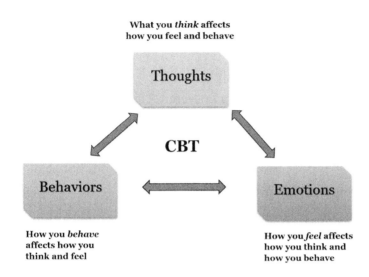

CBT espouses that our thoughts, emotions, and behaviors are all inexorably linked. As such, the thoughts you have about a situation can give rise to specific emotions, which in turn can result in behavior that may not be productive.

The cycle can work in other directions, too. For instance, if you display a new, positive behavior—one you may not have tried before—you may find that you think and feel more positively about a situation than you used to.

THE CORE PRINCIPLES OF CBT

The main principles of CBT are as follows:

1. Unhelpful ways of thinking can result in psychological problems.
2. Unhelpful beliefs can result in psychological problems.
3. Patterns of unhelpful behavior can result in psychological difficulties.
4. People who are battling psychological issues can learn better ways of coping, thus relieving their symptoms and achieving their personal and professional goals. CBT is not just about improving symptoms but also about solving problems on a long-term basis. Through this therapy, you can learn to identify flaws in your thinking patterns and amend them so you rely more on facts rather than on erroneous beliefs.

EFFECTIVE CBT STRATEGIES

Just a few of the many effective strategies employed in CBT include[26]:

- learning to identify cognitive distortions (These are harmful filters that can lead us to see people or situations in a negative light, even though we lack the evidence we need to come to the conclusions we do. We will delve deeply into cognitive distortions in Chapter Four.)

---

26 American Psychological Association, n.d.

- gaining a better understanding of others' motivations and behavior
- using problem-solving skills to solve challenging situations
- learning to become more confident in your own abilities
- changing behavior patterns by learning to calm your body and mind through mindfulness relaxation.
- learning to face your fears head-on, so you can overcome them

using role-playing to practice obtaining positive outcomes during challenging interactions with others

CBT empowers you to heal yourself. When you see a therapist, they give you "homework" or worksheets so that you can understand the thought-emotion-behavior link better. By completing these worksheets, you can learn more about beliefs or thought patterns that are standing in the way of your personal happiness and your relationships.

For instance, through regular journaling and CBT homework, you may discover that when you get angry, you "ghost" the people who have upset you. Others may have let you know how painful this is. If you keep displaying this behavior, some loved ones may tire of having the proverbial door shut in their face, and they may walk away. As such, you may decide to experiment with another behavior instead of ghosting.

For instance, if you need some time alone, you may let the other person know this, but get back to them within a stipulated time, so they do not feel like they are being punished or "in the dog house" because they disagreed with you or did not behave the way you wanted.

The ultimate goal of CBT is to enable you to think and behave in a way that benefits your mental health and well-being, strengthening healthy bonds with others. In order to do so, you need to be aware of how tense situations can provoke thoughts and feelings that lead you to make decisions. Without this awareness, you cannot stop automatic thoughts from leading you into undesired actions.

HOW YOUR THOUGHTS CAN AFFECT YOUR EMOTIONS AND BEHAVIORS

Below is an example of how negative thoughts can unleash emotions that lead to unproductive behavior. Beneath, we will discuss how you can use CBT to achieve a different outcome.

The Situation: A Successful Presentation

Your boss asked you and another colleague to pitch a marketing campaign to important clients. You were worried about this day because although you and your colleague created and worked on the entire campaign, public speaking makes you nervous, and you fear you might fumble or forget to make a specific point. Worst of all, you're worried your mind will go blank if the client asks you a question.

You've practiced hard for your pitch, role-playing your talk with your partner and colleagues many times, summarizing your thoughts into speech cards, and memorizing your main points so well that you don't need any prompts or notes during your presentation.

You do a mindfulness exercise before you head to work and tell yourself that even if the very worst thing happens (for instance, forgetting a point and having to look at your memory cards), it won't be the end of the world. You'll still have your job, your colleague will help you, and you can send them your report after your speech to ensure they have all the main points.

You do brilliantly! The hard work pays off, the client loves the idea, and they buy your campaign.

You should be happy, right? Except you're not. Here comes a negative thought that puts a damper on what should be a successful day. Your thought is: *I was extremely lucky this time. Next time I won't do as well.* This thought taps into your biggest insecurities, and you begin to doubt your self-worth. Your colleague suggests that you celebrate afterward, but you don't feel like it because you are worried about the follow-up meeting with the client and whether you'll be able to pull it off next time. You now feel worried, anxious, and angry at yourself. You wish you were as adept at public speaking as your colleague, who is the very picture of confidence when they deal with clients.

Through CBT, you will notice that you tend to use a specific "filter" when things go well: that of disqualifying the positive. This recognition can enable you to be on guard the next time an automatic put-down arises in your head.

You can then acknowledge your negative thoughts but think back to specific situations in the past (evidence) that show it is false. For instance, you might recall another successful presentation, your boss's grateful words, or the fact that your idea brought a lucrative client into your company!

HOW TO GAIN CONTROL OVER YOUR THOUGHTS AND EMOTIONS

When you repeatedly use the same negative filters, it is very difficult to notice what you are doing to yourself when you allow them to dominate your mood and determine your course of action. The following strategies can help you take the reins of your thoughts and emotions.

Give Yourself Time to Think

When a situation such as the example above arises, take some time to analyze how you went from a positive to a negative state. Write down the situation and the thoughts that ran through your mind. In this example, the specific thoughts could be:

- I lucked out this time.
- I'll never do this well next time.
- I forgot to mention an important point.
- My colleague, James, is such a natural. He made them laugh and was so relaxed when they asked us questions. I must have looked like a fool by his side.

Learn to Recognize Your Emotions

Think about the above thoughts and the emotions they produce. For instance, you might feel angry with yourself, sad, embarrassed, ashamed, envious, and anxious.

Focus on Changing Your Thoughts

In order to change your thoughts, you need to analyze the evidence that is available to you. What makes you think you lucked out and will do terribly next time? The current evidence is that you worked hard on a creative idea your clients liked, practiced your speech numerous times, thought up questions they might ask beforehand, and prepared your answers. Finally, your boss congratulated you and your colleague for a job well done.

Given the above evidence, try to think of what a reasonable person would think of your performance. They would probably think that, in your shoes, they would be happy with the outcome.

Given this evidence, you can focus on thinking more productive thoughts, such as:

- My hard work had the desired result.
- I can prepare in the same way for my next meeting with the client.
- I am sure that the more I practice speaking in public, the more comfortable I will be.

- My colleague, James, and I make a great team because I enjoy research, and he enjoys liaising with clients. We play off each other's strengths.

Understand That You Can Control Your Behavior

You have a choice as to whether you allow your negative filters to bring you so low that you don't feel like celebrating or you don't, instead taking your friend up on the offer and rewarding yourselves for a stellar job. Sometimes, even if you have doubts, choosing a positive behavior can have surprisingly good results. That is, once you're out, you may have such a great time with your colleague that you go home thinking about what an outstanding team you make. This can inspire you to start working on your next project together.

HOW YOUR BEHAVIORS CAN AFFECT YOUR THOUGHTS AND EMOTIONS

CBT isn't only about reframing your thoughts; it also involves trying new behaviors to serve you better and enhance relationships. The following behaviors can negatively affect your mental health[27].

Engaging in Negative Thought Patterns

We have shown how powerful negative thoughts can be and how they can lead you to discount all the positive aspects of a situation. If your mind tends to focus on the negative, know you're not alone! The human brain is hardwired to think

---

27 Bennett, 2018.

predominantly negative thoughts since doing so can ensure we have our defenses up when things actually go wrong.

However, negative thinking can become a pattern, and it can do us more harm than good, leading us to quit before we even start the race. When you find yourself thinking negative thoughts, remember the words of psychologist Jisun Fisher. She invites people to watch their thoughts assiduously before they are converted into beliefs. She states: "Our beliefs become dictators to how we show up in the world. And how we show up in the world inevitably leads us to the end-of-life question: 'Did I live a good life without regrets?'[28]"

Doing too Many Things at Once

Whether you are at work or spending your leisure time with family, try to be fully present. Put your phone down, stop checking your email, and don't take turns between working and watching YouTube videos. Taking on too many activities at once can increase stress levels and throw your concentration off.

Spending too Much Time on Social Media

The average person in the U.S. spends over two hours a day on social media and checks their phone over 340 times[29]! While connecting with friends is a de-stressor for many people, over-doing it can have the opposite effect. Many studies have found that using social media frequently is linked to a heightened risk of anxiety, depression, loneliness, and self-harm.

---

28 Bennett, 2018.
29 Content Works, 2022.

Social media can contribute to these problems because it sets unreasonable standards, invites comparisons with others, promotes FOMO (fear of missing out), increases the feeling of loneliness, and, in some cases, opens users up to cyberbullying or tense confrontations. The media is additionally filled with examples of people who have been seriously injured because they engaged in risky behavior to get Likes. Finally, social media use at night can disrupt your sleep since the light from your screen makes you more alert[30].

Procrastinating

Studies show that around 20 percent of adults procrastinate chronically, and between 80 and 90 percent of college students do so[31]. Putting off what you know you should be doing now can lead to feelings of anxiety and guilt. It can make you judge yourself as unproductive, lazy, and ineffectual[32].

Failing to Prioritize Your Physical Health

Daily exercise and quality sleep can dramatically reduce stress and anxiety levels. Yet the average person sleeps less than seven hours nightly[33]. This problem is echoed in many other countries, including the UK, other European countries, and Australia.

Meanwhile, only half of all adults meet officially recommended quotas for physical activity, as set by the Centers for Disease Control and Prevention[34]. Study after study has shown that exercise can help reduce the symptoms of depres-

---

30 Robinson & Smith, n.d.
31 Shatz, n.d.
32 The University of Kansas, n.d.
33 Single Care, 2023.
34 Kekatos, 2023.

sion and anxiety, boost your mood, and enhance your ability to focus.

Failing to Embrace a Growth Mindset

You can navigate life in a fixed or a growth mindset. People with a growth mindset believe that even though they may not have certain skills, abilities, or talents now, they can develop them through hard work and effort. When they fail, they try to find important life lessons since they see failure as part and parcel of growth.

People with a fixed mindset, on the other hand, believe that we are all born with natural skills, abilities, and talents. Failing at something they are supposed to be good at is disastrous for them because they define themselves in terms of these abilities. They also believe that if they aren't naturally good at something now, they never will be.

Which mindset do you think you should employ when you are working to heal your inner child?

HOW TO DEVELOP A GROWTH MINDSET

To harness the power of the growth mindset, try to[35]:

- Embrace challenges and see the opportunity they provide for growth.
- Persevere, even when you face setbacks.
- Know that you can continually increase your set of skills, talents, and abilities.

35 Wooll, 2021.

- Know that your intelligence can continue to grow throughout your lifetime.
- Let the success of others inspire you.
- Grab every opportunity you have to learn and experience new things.
- Accept criticism. It provides vital insight you can use to be your best self.

HOW TO BREAK BAD HABITS

If you find that you frequently engage in harmful behaviors, turn them around in the following ways:

- Avoid tempting situations. If social media is your bugbear, for instance, then remove a few apps from your phone, set a time limit for social media use, and make it a point to remember that what you see online doesn't necessarily reflect reality.
- Replace unhealthy behaviors with healthy ones. List two or three healthy behaviors you can commit to and do so strictly. You might commit to eating five portions of fruit a day, for instance, or going for a thirty-minute brisk walk daily.
- Prepare mentally for upcoming tasks and responsibilities. When you have a task to complete, break it up into smaller ones and set time limits for achieving each stage of your goal.
- Get support from the people you love, or seek professional help from a therapist.

. Celebrate small victories and reward yourself for them. Rewards can range from watching your favorite show to celebrating with a fancy dinner.

. Ask yourself why you really want to change. This will enable you to keep your eyes on the prize.

. Know that success doesn't look like a straight line[36]. Harness the power of the growth mindset and know that making mistakes is part and parcel of being human.

THE LINK BETWEEN ATTITUDE AND BEHAVIOR

Your attitude can have a positive or negative impact on your behavior. For instance, if you have a positive attitude toward your work, getting along with your colleagues, motivating them, and being more productive is easier. If you arrive at work with a negative attitude (you show apathy, boredom, and lack of interest), others are less likely to be attracted by your personality, and they will not be as interested in getting to know you, working alongside you, or asking for your opinion.

It also works the other way around. By embracing positive behaviors, your attitude can improve. This was proven in a now-iconic experiment known as the "Zimbardo study." In the study, researchers converted the basement of the Stanford University psychology building into a "prison." They chose 21 volunteers who were judged to be the most physically and mentally stable of the group who applied to take part in the study. The participants were assigned to play the role of either a prisoner or guard. The "prisoners" were arrested in their homes, fingerprinted, blindfolded, and taken to the prison.

36 Calechman, 2022.

Their quarters were small and had barred doors and bare walls. They were treated as prisoners usually are when they arrive in prison. For instance, they were stripped naked, and their possessions were taken away.

The guards wore typical uniforms and were instructed to do whatever they deemed necessary to maintain law and order in the prison. However, no physical violence was permitted.

Researchers note that a few hours after the experiment began, the guards started harassing the prisoners. The latter also behaved stereotypically, telling tales about other prisoners to the guards, talking about prison issues, and taking rules very seriously, to the point of siding with the guards against those who broke the rules.

There were many more mishaps, and some of the prisoners experienced emotional breakdowns. As such, although the experiment was supposed to last for two weeks, it was called off after six days owing to the prisoners' emotional state and the guards' aggressiveness.

The study demonstrated that people quickly play the roles that society expects them to, especially when these roles are stereotypical. In other words, people can become so immersed in social norms that they lose their sense of identity and personal responsibility[37].

It also revealed that by engaging in specific behaviors (for instance, playing a role you've been "assigned"), you can shape your attitude toward situations and people. The experiment is a vital reminder to question your behavior and keep yourself in

37 McLeod, 2023.

check. The experiment also highlights that the different roles you play (in your family, at work, and in social settings) shape how you are likely to act. Still, you can go against the grain and embrace more positive behaviors. Knowing yourself and working on behaviors that are out of line with your core values are aspects that cognitive behavioral therapy can help you out with.

DANIEL KATZ'S FOUR ATTITUDE CLASSIFICATIONS

When analyzing your attitude toward everything from work to social situations, it can be helpful to take renowned psychologist Daniel Katz's four attitude classifications into account. Katz stipulated that the purpose of attitudes is to mediate between your needs (like safety or self-expression) and the external environment. You adopt specific attitudes to help you meet your needs in some way or another. Katz identified four needs that human attitudes fulfill[38]:

1. The adaptive function is an attitude that helps you achieve a goal or evade undesirable consequences. An example of the adaptive function is dressing a particular way or listening to a specific type of music to fit in with your group, or maybe you back your local football team so your friends don't protest.
2. The knowledge function is an attitude you adopt to make the world more understandable, predictable, or knowable to you. Examples of the knowledge function in action are the generally accepted stereotypes about people. Accepting these makes it easier to make sense of

---

38 Psycholotron, n.d.

people quickly, but in the long run, it can make your assessment of them inaccurate.

3. The value-expressive function is an attitude you take to express the values that are inextricably linked to your self-concept. An example of the value-expressive function is assigning value to a specific religious symbol because it is connected to important spiritual matters. Another is buying a specific brand of car because it is associated with elegance or sophistication.

4. The ego-defense function is an attitude you adopt to protect yourself from psychologically damaging events. For instance, an older manager whose decisions are continually challenged by an entry-level manager may label the latter as cocky, immature, and unskilled.

When you find yourself expressing a strong or sustained attitude toward people or situations, think about what function your attitude may be fulfilling. Think about whether these attitudes are productive or not and how you might benefit from positive change.

3 INTRODUCTORY CBT ACTIVITIES

It's now time to pull your journal out and try three beginner CBT activities.

Fact or Opinion

Learning to differentiate between facts and opinions is an important part of evidence gathering for CBT. The difference between the two is that facts can be verified. Opinions are personal interpretations of facts, and they differ from person to person. Your brain sometimes finds it hard to differentiate the two, so remind it to do so often[39].

In this exercise, decide if the following are facts or opinions:

1. I am a good listener.
2. I am intelligent.
3. My hair is straight.
4. My boss is a terrible leader.
5. We sold more than any other sales team this quarter.
6. Sam is angry at me, and I know this because they were very serious today.
7. People didn't enjoy my presentation today.
8. I'm not as funny as my friend Kim.
9. My boss said I couldn't have a raise yet.
10. I spent two hours on social media today.

(Answers: 1-opinion, 2-opinion, 3-fact, 4-opinion, 5-fact, 6-opinion, 7-opinion, 8-opinion, 9-fact, 10-fact).

Performing a Functional Analysis

When identifying behaviors or habits that could be causing you harm, it can help to conduct a functional analysis. This involves studying the ABCs of an event: the antecedent, behavior, and consequence. To help with inner child healing, conduct this analysis by answering the following four questions in your journal[40]:

39 Therapist Aid, n.d.
40 Compitus, 2020.

- What situation triggered a negative thought or emotion? Example: A person you are interested in said no when you asked them on a date.
- What thoughts did this situation provoke? Example: It provoked thoughts like, I am unlovable. I'm not attractive enough for someone like them to date. I'm boring.
- What behavior resulted from the trigger and thought? Example: I stayed home and binged on unhealthy food instead of going out that night.
- What was the consequence of this behavior? Example: My friends had a great night out and met many new people.

✎...

✎...

✎...

✎...

Actual and Alternate Thoughts

Think about the automatic thoughts that arise when you face challenging situations. Try to replace negative automatic thoughts with alternative, positive ones. Do the same for your feelings and behaviors.

For example:

Situation: My colleague wasn't as friendly today as she normally is.
Actual Thought: She's probably mad at me.
Alternate Thought: She's probably so busy she didn't even notice I was there.
Negative Emotion: I'm hurt and angry.
Positive Emotion: I'm okay with it/ I'm not bothered.
Negative Behavior: I go to her desk angrily, demanding an explanation.
Positive Behavior: I wait until she has more time to have a coffee or lunch and enjoy our usual bonding time.

Situation: My boyfriend didn't text me today.
Actual Thought: He must be with that attractive colleague of his again.
Alternate Thought: He could be seeing many clients today.
Negative Emotion: I feel jealous and abandoned.
Positive Emotion: I am not bothered.
Negative Behavior: I rage text him.
Positive Behavior: I text him letting him know that I am thinking about him and wishing him success in meeting his sales target for the day.

Situation: My friend didn't stand up for me when I was arguing with another friend.

Actual Thought: He is disloyal.

Alternative Thought: Perhaps he prefers that we sort things out ourselves.

Negative Emotion: I am angry at him.

Positive Emotion: I respect his views on the importance of avoiding friendship triangles.

Negative Behavior: I berate my friend for not sticking up for me.

Positive Behavior: I let him know that I respect the fact that he thinks we should make peace without third parties getting involved.

✎…

✎…

✎…

✎…

Now that you understand how your thoughts, emotions, and behaviors interact and influence each other, it's time to get to the first step of the five-step method for healing your inner child: reframing the thoughts that are causing pain.

4

STEP 1: REFRAME THE THOUGHTS THAT HURT YOUR INNER CHILD

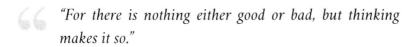

"For there is nothing either good or bad, but thinking makes it so."

— SHAKESPEARE

The National Science Foundation reports that 80 percent of our thoughts are negative, and 95 percent are repetitive. When you partake in negative thinking, it can cause significant damage to your inner child. It can make it harder for you to trust others, despite the fact that reaching out to friends and family is a powerful way to heal trauma. Investing time in reframing negative thoughts will enable you to see situations (and others' intentions) in a more positive light. This will lead to new behaviors that will enrich your relationships and experiences.

SHANE

Shane had a couple of good friends that had been in his life since childhood—so much so that they were like family. Whenever Shane had a problem, he could pick up the phone or connect online with his friends, even though they lived in different cities. Shane was very grateful for them but found that making new friends was much harder once he moved to a new city for work.

The friendships he made in adulthood were more fleeting and superficial, and it made him feel insecure. For instance, he had a few friends at work but noticed that if one left the job or got sent to another office, they would no longer keep in touch. Shane had another issue: he found it hard to interpret others' behaviors at his new workplace. It seemed that others were making fun of him or excluding him from their conversations.

Shane had had this same sensation at other workplaces. He was introverted and found interpreting others' words and body language hard. He often assumed he wasn't liked and accepted, leading him to shun any attempts at integrating him into a group. Meanwhile, his colleagues felt the complete opposite. They wanted to get to know him, but if they included him in office banter and humor, he seemed to take it personally. They slowly tired of trying to make him feel at home. Their team had always been one big happy family, and a few were concerned about what they could do to make Shane feel more like a part of it.

HOW CAN YOUR THOUGHTS HURT YOUR INNER CHILD?

We mentioned in Chapter Three how CBT works by helping you reframe negative thoughts. When someone's thoughts are primarily negative, it is a sign that their hurt inner child is surfacing. Lawyer and blogger Gray Robinson divides thoughts into four types. This categorization is very pertinent to inner child work[41].

The Inner Critic

The inner critic is the person that tells you that you could do better, you need help, or you are struggling with a task. Your inner critic can be a positive force in your life. They help you identify areas that can benefit from a different approach or more consistent work.

However, when this voice takes on a more negative tinge, it can interfere with your goals and damage your well-being. This negative voice might sound something like this: "You're hopeless." "You always f things up." "You'll never be as successful as ___." The difference between positive and negative criticism is that the former inspires or motivates you to improve. The latter makes you feel hopeless, stuck, and incapable of improvement.

The Ego

Robinson points out the positive and negative aspects of the ego or self. Examples of positive ego include, "I feel confident in

----
41 Robinson, n.d.

my job," "I work hard," or "I complete my tasks on time." Examples of negative ego are, "I don't deserve to do well." "I just can't do this," or "My life is so hard."

The Inner Child

Your positive inner child is at play when you are having the time of your life. That sense of giddy joy you get when you jump into the sea, toast s'mores over a roaring fire, or order your favorite childhood ice cream flavor are what enjoying life is all about. On the other hand, a hurt inner child can resurface in tough moments through emotions and actions such as fear, insecurity, and the mislabelling of others' intentions.

Inspired Thought

Inspiration comes when you are freed from your negative inner critic, ego, and inner child. When positive thoughts emerge, you can come up with creative solutions to problems. Inner thoughts, Robinson notes, play a key role when you face adverse or unexpected events. If you assume failure, you are less likely to take the steps you need to succeed.

Your thoughts are influenced by your subconscious mind, trauma, physical health, and other factors. The good news is that you can change the way you think. By doing so, you will find that your experiences become more positive.

COGNITIVE DISTORTIONS

One of the first steps in thinking more positively involves identifying the cognitive distortions that stand in the way of your personal and professional goals.

As I mentioned in Chapter Three, cognitive distortions are internal mental filters or biases that result in greater anxiety, sadness, and feelings of poor self-worth. Knowing what they are and identifying the filters you use in your own life are important parts of inner child healing.

10 Common Cognitive Distortions

Some of the most typical cognitive distortions people employ to create a more predictable world include the following.

1. Black-and-White (All-or-Nothing) Thinking[42]

- *"I never feel happy."*
- *"Everything is terrible."*
- *"Things will always be this tough."*
- *"My friend let me down today. That means they are a bad friend."*
- *"If something bad happened today, it's a bad day."*

2. Jumping to Conclusions (Mind-Reading)

- *"She didn't smile at me today. She mustn't like me."*
- *"My boss didn't answer my email asking about a project. He's trying to show he's in control by making me wait."*

42 Arocho, 2022.

- *"He didn't invite me to his party. He's trying to push me out of my new group."*
- *"She didn't say she liked my new boyfriend. She must be jealous of me."*
- *"I haven't heard from Janina in two weeks. She must be angry at me."*

3. Personalization

- *"My team lost because I missed that goal."*
- *"Our group project got a lower grade than the winning group because of my work."*
- *"My friend canceled the plan with me because they don't enjoy spending time with me."*
- *"If I had been there, I would have stopped that car from crashing into my friend's."*
- *"The teacher got mad at the class today because of me."*

4. Should-ing and Must-ing

- *"I should lose weight."*
- *"I should always put others first."*
- *"I must be in control of situations."*
- *"I should never say no to others."*
- *"I should exercise more."*

5. Focusing on the Negative

- *"My boss said my project was good, but that I should work on the design."* (Focusing on the one bad thing he said instead of all his positive feedback)
- *"I'm incapable of sticking to my exercise routine."* (I didn't work out one day but worked out four days this week.)
- *"She said she was interested in me but wanted to wait before calling me her boyfriend."* (Worrying that the person will not commit to them instead of being happy the person loves them)
- *"She liked my dress but said I should try wearing it with a belt."* (She must think the dress made me look like a sack of potatoes.)
- *"My partner said our budget wasn't big enough to go to Melbourne when we vacation this year."* (Even though the partner said they could afford to go to three other cities in Australia on their available budget)

6. Overgeneralization

- *"I'll never meet my soulmate."*
- *"I'll never get fit."*
- *"I'll never get an A in math."*
- *"I'm never going to make good friends."*
- *"I'm a complete failure at work."*

7. Magnification and Minimization (Emphasizing the Negative While Minimizing the Positive)

- *"My boss asked me to correct my article. They don't appreciate me."* (Ignoring the fact the boss praised many other parts of the article and asked for a change in one paragraph)
- *"I spilled that drink. Now everyone at the party thinks I'm an idiot."* (Despite the fact everyone enjoyed your company and didn't care about the drink)
- *"They told me I looked good. They're just being nice. I know I look terrible."*
- *"I don't deserve the praise. Anyone could have done it."* (After achieving a major accomplishment)
- *"I achieved a great time at the track today, but it was because I had a lucky day."*

8. Fortune-Telling

- *"My sugar levels will show I have diabetes."*
- *"I will be the first one fired."*
- *"He will dump me."*
- *"The same disaster that happened to___will occur to me."*
- *"That promotion will go to someone else."*

9. Catastrophizing (Blowing Things out of Proportion)

- *"This pain in my leg is probably a blood clot."*
- *"Sheena didn't invite me to her party. She's going to cut me out of the friend group now."*

- *"I failed one exam. I'm a terrible person."*

10. Labeling

- *"I'm not a healthy person."*
- *"I'm not a go-getter."*
- *"I'm anti-social."*
- *"I'm too introverted."*
- *"I'm not as charming as____."*

Many of these distortions have one thing in common: they tend to assume things and intentions without the evidence required to make such serious or devastating conclusions. The next time an automatic negative thought pops into your head, try to think about which type of filter you are using. Try to notice if you tend to use some filters more than others.

HOW TO IDENTIFY AND REPLACE NEGATIVE THINKING PATTERNS

The next time you catch one of these negative thoughts in action, put the following strategy into place:

1. Stop and recognize negative thoughts when they arise.

The negative thought you caught: *I'm too lazy to stick to my exercise routine.*

2. Identify your thinking traps.

I'm labeling myself.

3. Challenge your negative thoughts with evidence.

I only missed one gym class this week because I caught a cold. I am capable of committing to my routine. What's more, there have been times in my life when I have exercised for two hours daily, and I have stuck to that tough routine for years. This shows I have grit, discipline, and determination.

4. Reframe these negative thoughts.

I am committed to achieving my fitness goal.

5. Journal your negative thoughts.

Write down the situation that made you have negative thoughts, refute them with evidence, and reframe them.

6. Exercise and meditate.

In the next section, we will delve into mindfulness and provide mindfulness exercises.

7. Ask yourself key questions.

Some questions you might ask yourself are:

- "Why do I say negative things to myself?"
- "Are these negative thoughts helpful?"
- "What positive things can I say to myself daily to counter the power of these negative thoughts?"

8. Practice acceptance.

Accept that all human beings make mistakes, but they are also capable of great things.

THE POWER OF MINDFULNESS

Mindfulness is a buzzword in health and wellness these days, but what does it actually mean, and how can you harness its power in your daily life?

Mindfulness is rooted in the practice of meditation. It involves detaching yourself from your thoughts and emotions and observing them from afar. Practicing mindfulness can help you become more conscious of your thoughts and build greater self-awareness. It can stop negative thought patterns and help you preserve your inner child's well-being.

Studies have shown that people who practice mindfulness have fewer negative thoughts after exposure to negative imagery[43]. This shows that it may lessen the impact of negative thinking.

---

43 Kiken & Shook, 2014.

Research has also revealed that it lights up parts of our brains that aren't usually activated when we're mindlessly running on autopilot[44].

Although mindful meditation is the most oft-mentioned means of embracing mindfulness, there are many other ways of doing so, including:

- paying attention to your senses
- living in the moment
- accepting yourself
- focusing on your breathing
- sitting meditation
- walking meditation

A BEGINNER'S MINDFUL MEDITATION EXERCISE

You can meditate practically anywhere, and you need little more than peace and quiet and a comfy spot to sit in. Below is a simple exercise you can perform in as little as five minutes. Of course, if you enjoy breathing exercises, you can always extend your breathing sessions.[45]

1. Start by finding a comfortable position (sitting or lying down).
2. Take a few deep breaths. Breathe in through your nose and out through your mouth.
3. Focus on your breath, noticing the rising and falling sensation. Simply observe how you breathe and the rise and fall of your breath.

44 Mindful, n.d.
45 Positive Psychology, n.d.

4. Focus on how the air passes through your nose, into your throat, and then your lungs, feeling the expansion of your chest and belly.

Do this for a few minutes.

A MEDITATION SCRIPT TO HEAL YOUR INNER CHILD

The following mindfulness script is one that is specifically centered on your inner child.

1. Sit in a comfortable, peaceful spot and take a big breath in and out.
2. Try to notice the tension in your body, starting in your toes and moving up toward your calves, thighs, belly, chest, hands, arms, neck, shoulders, and head. Squeeze the muscles in each of these parts, then relax them and try to imagine that all the tension has gone away.
3. Imagine that your body is now very heavy, and you are deeply relaxed.
4. Your inner child now visits you. Try to notice everything you can about them. Notice what they are wearing, if they are smiling or serious, what their hair is like, etc.
5. Imagine what they are feeling.

- They may wish they were more loved.
- They may wish they felt more secure.
- They may wish someone defended them.

- They may wish they could trust others.

6. Inhale deeply, and as you exhale, blow those negative emotions away.
7. Take the child, embrace them warmly, and feel love in your heart as you hold them. Watch those thoughts leave their mind. Tell them, "I love you. I accept you. I will protect you."

BREATHING TECHNIQUES TO HEAL YOUR INNER CHILD

Breathing techniques are powerful tools you can harness to heal your inner child. Studies have shown that controlled breathing lowers stress hormones dramatically. It can also stop a panic attack in its tracks.

Research by Florida Atlantic University scientists has found that paced breathing stimulates the vagus nerve (which regulates the heart rate and respiratory rate) and parasympathetic nervous system (which relaxes your body after periods of stress or danger)[46]. This reduces the stress chemicals in your brain and lowers blood pressure. This is powerful stuff, considering the fact that over 100 million Americans have high blood pressure, and high blood pressure is linked to strokes and heart attacks.

----

46 Brenner et al., 2020.

Alternate Nose Breathing

This type of breathing has been found to lower your heart rate and improve cardiovascular functions. It is a good option when you are anxious or stressed and your heart is racing[47].

1. Sit in a comfortable spot.
2. Take your right hand and bend your pointer and middle fingers inward toward your palm so they are out of the way.
3. Close your nostril with your right thumb, and inhale through the left nostril.
4. Close your left nostril with your ring finger, and exhale through the right nostril.
5. Inhale through the right, and exhale through the left.

Repeat steps 1. to 5. a few times.

Equal Breathing

This breathing technique is centered on inhaling and exhaling for the same amount of time. Like alternate breathing, it helps lower stress and create a sense of balance[48].

1. Sit in a comfortable position.
2. Inhale and exhale through your nose.
3. Count during each inhalation and exhalation, ensuring you spend the same number of seconds on each.
4. You can add a natural pause between each breath.

47 Introsport, 2018.
48 Cronkleton, 2023.

Continue for around five minutes.

POSITIVE AFFIRMATIONS

After reframing your thoughts, it can help to reward yourself with positive affirmations that will give you a welcome buzz and make you feel more positive as you make your way through the world. Positive affirmations have been shown to reduce negative thoughts because they boost self-awareness of negative patterns and feelings. This makes it harder for negative thoughts to wreak havoc on your mental health and happiness.

You can use a wealth of affirmations, but creating your own meaningful ones is best. Once you do, write them on Post-its or make a poster and put them up in a place where you can see them regularly. Examples of positive affirmations include[49]:

- "I am looking after my inner child."
- "I am listening to my inner child's voice."
- "My inner child deserves to be heard."
- "My vulnerability is my strength."
- "I love my inner child unconditionally."
- "I exercise self-care daily."
- "I treat myself with compassion."
- "My mistakes do not define me. They allow me to grow."
- "I take care of my body."
- "I find ways to protect my mental health."
- "I have a beautiful light within me."
- "I am a hard worker."

49 Gratitude Blog, n.d.

- "I give myself to others."
- "I am doing the best I can."

POSITIVE SELF-TALK

Back up your inspiring positive affirmations with positive self-talk. Imagine how powerful they can be against the onslaught of automatic negative thoughts that cause constant damage to your inner child. The benefits of speaking to yourself positively include:

- better self-esteem
- reduced symptoms of depression, anxiety, and personality disorders
- a sense that you are in control of your life
- help with chronic pain
- greater motivation to overcome obstacles
- finding it easier to calm down

Strategies to Talk to Yourself Positively

Throughout your day, remember to[50]:

- Think good things about yourself. See the glass as half-full.
- Try to exercise gratitude.
- Identify your strengths.
- Accept compliments.
- Look, think, and act positively.

----

50 Health Direct, n.d.

Try to turn negative self-talk into positive or neutral self-talk

Examples of Negative vs. Positive Self-Talk:

Negative Self-Talk	Positive Talk
This task or problem is impossible.	This sounds like a good challenge.
I can't do this.	I will try to do this and give it my all.
I always make mistakes.	I have so many things to learn from my mistakes.
Nobody likes me here.	I like myself.
I don't know anything about this.	I am keen to learn.

THE POWER OF POSITIVE INFLUENCES

Think about your inner child and the hurt you could cause them by surrounding yourself with people who take advantage of their vulnerability. Spend time with positive people and try to consume books and media that inspire you to treat yourself better. Take part in activities that uplift your mind and strengthen your body.

Positive influences can include:

- poetry and films that inspire you
- friends who accept you for who you are and who always have your best intentions at heart
- family members who respect your boundaries and support your projects, hopes, and dreams
- a life coach or mentor who can guide you on your path to doing great things

- a colleague who lends a helping hand at work
- anyone who strengthens your belief in yourself

Think about the people you currently spend time with.

- Do they listen to you actively and take your feelings into account?
- Do they allow you to express your vulnerability?
- Do they share their own vulnerability with you?
- Do they leave you with a happy feeling after seeing them?
- Do they make you feel liked and loved?
- Do they make you feel like they think you are funny, wise, and a good friend?
- Do they inspire you with their words or deeds?

3 CBT EXERCISES FOR REFRAMING THOUGHTS TO HEAL YOUR INNER CHILD

Challenging Negative Thoughts

The goal of this exercise is to reframe negative thoughts into positive ones. It is undertaken with a journal[51].

What is the situation causing me hurt, pain, or stress?

Example: A friend had a cocktail party and didn't invite me.

----
51 Pangilinan, 2022.

What are the thoughts that entered my mind when I encountered this situation?

They can't stand me. They are trying to shut me out. I'll have to look for a new set of friends. These people think they're too good for me. They are awful and ungenerous.

Is there substantial evidence for my thought?

- Do you know why your friend threw the party?
- Did they invite everyone else in your friend group except you?
- Do they normally treat you poorly, or do they show you they value you in other ways?
- Have they invited you to other social events?

Is there evidence against my thought?

My friend often tells me how important I am to them. They may have invited people who were exclusively tied to work or a specific project they are undertaking. It may be a small party, and they may have limited space. Is it possible I don't have all the evidence I need to interpret this situation?

How could I look at this situation more positively/What positive thoughts can counter my negative automatic thoughts?

We all have different groups of friends. Sometimes, I enjoy being with my work group. At others, I hang around parents from school. I also organize meet-ups that do not involve everyone.

How do I feel when I see this in a more positive light?

I feel liberated. I feel like I don't need to control the decisions my friends make. So long as they are there when I need them, we connect once in a while, and they treat me with respect and kindness, I am fulfilled.

Will this situation still be important to me in a week, a month, or a year?

In a month, I will probably have seen them in other social settings, and everything will be fine.

✎...

✎...

✎...

✎...

Finding My Core Belief

Often, the automatic negative thoughts that run through your mind affirm the negative core beliefs that are hurting your inner child. You can use these thoughts to discover your core belief while also resolving to move your mind from negative to positive.

What is the situation that is causing me to feel bad?

I can't afford to buy the car I want.

What automatic negative thoughts ran through my head?

I should be earning more money. All my other friends can afford expensive cars.

What belief do these thoughts reflect?

I am a failure.

How do they make me feel?

They make me feel sad, frustrated, and angry.

What am I doing about it?

Sitting at home overthinking about how devoid of quality and happiness my life is.

What can I do about it?

I can look for a more affordable car.
I can get a part-time job.
I can find freelance work—for instance, I can write a blog,
work as a virtual personal assistant, or do some editing.

✎...

✎...

✎...

✎...

Your belief is actually stopping you from moving in the direction of achieving your goals because it leads to worry, rumination, and stagnation. In Chapter 5, you will discover how to reframe negative core beliefs, but for now, it pays to be aware of the link between your beliefs and your thoughts.

Solve the Problem

A powerful way to nip negative thoughts in the bud is to embrace a strategy that solves the problem you are facing. Once you embark on a proactive path to ending your cause of anxiety, sadness, or anger, you realize that you are much more in control of your life than you ever realized.

What is the problem?

My husband will be abroad for work on my birthday.

What negative automatic thoughts arise?

He doesn't care enough about me. He cares more about pleasing his boss than about me. This is a special moment for me, and I'm throwing a party I would like him to attend.

What will happen if I keep thinking these thoughts?

Our relationship will become strained, and we will keep arguing.

What positive thoughts can replace the negative ones?

He loves me and works so hard so we can have a good life, pay for our home, and take wonderful vacations together. I also work hard and sometimes work late because I have similar goals, and he is understanding during these times.

What are some possible solutions to this problem?

I can throw my party when he's back.
I can go through with my arrangements and organize a live call with him so everyone can say hi.
I can plan a special celebration just for us two when he gets back.

✎...

✎...

✎...

You are now fully in tune with the way that negative thoughts can bring you down and potentially cause great damage to your mental health. You know how to change these thoughts around using the information and exercises in this chapter. Your core beliefs can also damage you and stop you from embarking upon healthy relationships. Discover more about core beliefs in the next chapter.

5

STEP 2: REFRAME THE BELIEFS THAT HURT YOUR INNER CHILD

"If our core belief is based on what other people think, then we eventually will allow their opinions to become our reality."

— DARREN JOHNSON

For many people, going against core beliefs is one of the most difficult parts of healing the inner child. It may seem easier to stop an automatic thought in your head than to challenge a poor sense of self-worth that you have harbored since childhood. However, working on your core beliefs is also one of the most rewarding parts of your journey. Once you identify them and stop them from defining you, your self-esteem will grow in abundance, and you will feel much more confident in various areas of your life.

MALIK

Malik grew up with parents who set very high standards for him. They expected him to "win" at everything, including academics and sports. If he got an A, they asked him why he hadn't received an A+. As an adult, Malik found it hard to take criticism and saw negative feedback as an attack on his identity. He wanted everyone to think he was perfect and spent so much time trying to achieve perfection that he often failed himself. His negative core beliefs led him to settle for less because he just didn't believe he was worthy of the very best jobs, relationships, and life experiences.

WHAT ARE NEGATIVE CORE BELIEFS, AND HOW ARE THEY FORMED?

Negative core beliefs are potentially harmful beliefs you have about yourself. They are usually based on negative experiences you may have encountered during your childhood.

Examples of negative core beliefs include:

- *"I am worthless."*
- *"I am inadequate."*
- *"I am a failure."*
- Your negative core beliefs can also be about other people. For instance:
- *"People are malicious."*
- *"People are untrustworthy."*
- *"All people are self-interested."*

- *"If I let others know about my life experiences, they will use this information to get back at me one day."*

FEATURES OF NEGATIVE CORE BELIEFS

Negative core beliefs tend to:

1. be absolutist or all-or-nothing in nature
2. be self-sustaining (Negative beliefs look for reasons to "prove" that they are true. They find these reasons in a myriad of interactions and settings, often assigning meanings and intentions that do not exist.)
3. overlook evidence that demonstrates their inaccuracy

HOW TO IDENTIFY NEGATIVE CORE BELIEFS

Negative core beliefs can also be difficult to identify because they have been ingrained in your mind since childhood. In order to identify your core beliefs, try to:

1. Notice themes in the way you think. If you find that you judge yourself or others frequently without taking time to use reliable standards for your judgment, your negative core beliefs are probably at work.
2. Use Socratic questions to uncover your core beliefs. These are questions that encourage reflection and problem-solving. When you use a blanket statement like, "I am not likable," ask yourself questions like, "What evidence is there for this?" "Is there any evidence

to the contrary?" "What life experiences could have led me to believe this about myself?"

3. Learn about typical negative core beliefs. In the exercise section of this chapter, we will provide you with a host of common negative beliefs. You can then circle those which are most pertinent to you.

4. Take a close look at your inner rules. Everyone has a unique set of rules they live by. Inner rules comprise our beliefs about what must happen for us to feel good about an experience. If___happens, I feel happy. However, any time our expectations aren't met, we fall into a state of unhappiness and respond from that negative state[52].

Typical inner rules include:

- *If I don't get promoted this year, I'm just not good enough at my job.*
- *If the client doesn't like my idea, I'm just not creative enough.*
- *If I don't get assigned that interesting project, it's because I'm older than the newer employees.*
- *If someone else gets promoted, my employers don't value me.*
- *If I don't improve my running time this month, I'm just not good enough to be on the team.*
- *I need to 'earn' happiness.*
- *My best efforts are not good enough.*
- *If I allow someone to really know me, they'll abandon me.*

Key Fact: Rules are not always negative. They can have a positive effect on your life. Examples of positive rules include:

52 The Relationship Guy, n.d.

- *When I'm angry at someone, it's important to speak directly to them instead of speaking to others.*
- *I won't start surfing on the Internet until my work is done.*
- *I will speak my truth to others but also be empathetic and listen to what they have to say.*

Rules become problematic when they become too restrictive or place too much pressure on you. The key question to ask yourself when you encounter an inner rule is, "Is this rule helping me and others, or is it hurting my inner child?"

HOW DO HARMFUL BELIEFS HURT YOUR INNER CHILD?

Harmful beliefs can have a profound impact on your inner child. They can make you feel that you're not good, intelligent, or worthy enough. They make your inner child feel rejected and unloved. They can additionally interfere with your inner child's willingness to show their vulnerability and take reasoned risks. Your inner child can become too cautious and avoid situations in which they can potentially get hurt.

12 STRATEGIES FOR CHALLENGING YOUR NEGATIVE CORE BELIEF SYSTEM

Recognizing your negative core beliefs and stopping them from interfering with your goals can, and often does, involve more than one strategy. Below are 12 powerful strategies to adopt:

Embrace self-compassion and self-acceptance

The words "self-compassion" may be misleading because we usually employ compassion in the sense of feeling sorry for someone or exercising empathy and understanding toward them.

Self-compassion can be defined as self-kindness or, more precisely, being as kind to yourself as you are to others. Studies have shown that this quality can be a powerful tool when it comes to battling the perfectionism and self-judgment that can hurt your inner child.

A Study on Self-Esteem

A 2007 Duke University study showed that treating yourself kindly when things go wrong is key when it comes to facing life's toughest challenges[53]. The researchers asked themselves, "Why do some people roll with the punches, facing problems with grace, while others buckle under?" The answer lies in self-compassion.

Being kind to yourself when things go wrong eliminates the anger, depression, and pain your hurt inner child can bring to the fore. When you are self-compassionate, you stop yourself from adding a layer of self-recrimination to the bad things that are already occurring. If you beat yourself up whenever you make a mistake or you fail, it becomes impossible to react non-defensively to your difficulties.

----

53 Science Daily, 2007.

Self-compassion allows you to separate your happiness from external events because you are always okay with yourself—in good and bad times.

This quality is particularly important for people with a hurt inner child or self-esteem issues. If you have low self-esteem but you treat yourself kindly, said the researchers, then you generally fare as well as someone with high self-esteem does.

Self-Compassion and Perfectionism

Self-compassion is also key when your inner child has been hurt because of others' (or your own) perfectionism. A 2018 study by scientists from the Australian Catholic University discovered that self-compassion could weaken the link between perfectionism and depression.

Practice Self-Care

Self-care is the buzzword in the health and wellness sector. It essentially embraces the wide array of actions you can undertake to prioritize your physical and mental health. Integrated self-care involves consuming healthy foods, exercising daily, battling stress proactively through mindfulness and activities such as yoga, and ensuring you get enough time outdoors.

It can also include pampering yourself once in a while. However, it is important to differentiate between a luxury spa day and authentic self-care. In order to be authentically kind to yourself, you need to make good decisions and lead a lifestyle that promotes peace, happiness, and fulfillment.

Embrace Effective Stress Management

Above, we spoke of the importance of tackling stress actively and regularly through stress-busting activities such as yoga or spending time in nature. It can also help to analyze the way you view and respond to stress. Many people make excuses to allow themselves to remain in a worried state[54]. They may:

- Justify stress as temporary.
- Think that high levels of stress are just another part of daily work or home life.
- Blame stress on other people or on outside events.

Scientifically Proven Ways to Manage Stress

Your stress management arsenal can include one or more strategies. Try the following techniques and pick and choose those you find most useful:

- Guided Imagery

A relaxation method that keeps your mind on positive images to reduce pain, stress, and other negative emotions. Guided imagery can be as simple as imagining yourself in a beach setting. Aim to add lots of details to your imagined scene. For instance, you might imagine the feel of the sea breeze, the smell of the salty air, or the feel of the sand beneath your feet.

----

54 Robinson & Smith, n.d.

- Progressive Muscle Relaxation

This activity involves tightening and relaxing muscles (from your toes to your head) to eliminate tension from the body and mind. Doing so enables you to discover where you hold tension in your body, so you can be more mindful of the way stress affects your physical well-being.

- Physical Affection

Hugging a loved one or a pet can release "feel-good" endorphins while also bonding us to others and helping strengthen our relationships.

- Aromatherapy

Essential oils such as lavender have been found to decrease stress and agitation. One study showed that lavender essential oil effectively ameliorated generalized anxiety disorder, similar to 0.5mg/daily of a popular benzodiazepine (a medication used to treat anxiety and related sleep problems)[55].

Essential oils are usually applied to the skin or diffused through an essential oil diffuser. Some oils can be consumed. (For instance, essential oils like peppermint and bergamot are sometimes added to desserts.) However, it is important to do your research beforehand since not all oils are comestible, and some can cause skin irritation unless they are diluted. Lavender, jasmine, and rose essential oils can all be applied to the skin

---

55 Braden et al., 2009.

though to play it extra-safe, dilute them in a carrier oil first (Kassim, 2022).

- Creativity

Research indicates that creativity helps reduce stress and promote relaxation. It also helps stave off age-related brain function decline[56]. You can also delve into the methods mentioned previously in this book—including mindfulness and controlled breathing.

- Stress-Relief Supplements

Some supplements may give you a helping hand with stress. You can start out with a multivitamin, which can address any nutritional deficiencies you may have. Additional supplements that have shown some evidence of success when it comes to stress relief include Ashwagandha (an adaptogenic herb thought to boost resilience to physical and mental stress), B vitamins (which have been found to improve mood and lower stress), melatonin (which can help regulate your body's circadian rhythm so you can get a good night's sleep), and L-theanine (an amino acid that can promote better sleep and relaxation)[57].

Seek Support From Others

For most people, spending time with people they connect with is a vital way to feel instantly reinvigorated, safe, and understood. While most people connect with others via social media,

----

56 Marobella, 2023.
57 Scott, 2022.

make sure to meet your friends in person once in a while too. Doing so releases a cascade of hormones that stops the body's "fight or flight" response from triggering anxiety or a panic attack[58].

Practice Gratitude

There are many ways to be grateful. For instance, you can say gratitude-based affirmations to yourself or use a journal to list the things in your life you are grateful for.

Reward Yourself Regularly

Celebrate the achievement of small and big goals alike. If you have placed considerable effort into a goal, reward yourself for your hard work, whether or not you actually achieve your goal.

Work With a Mental Health Professional

If your inner child is hurting to such an extent that you are struggling with your work or personal relationships, a therapist can help clarify your path and share useful strategies to see life in a more positive light.

----
58 Help Guide, n.d.

Keep a Stress Journal

When you feel stressed, take your journal and answer the following questions:

- What triggered your stress?
- How did you feel physically, emotionally, and mentally?
- How did you respond?
- What did you do to self-soothe?

Embrace the 4 As of stress management[59]

1. Avoid unnecessary stressors if you can. Your list of stressors can include people, situations, and hot topics.
2. Alter the situation. Change the way you communicate when a stressor arises. You may decide to talk about your emotions instead of keeping them inside, be more assertive, and/or be willing to give and take in your relationships.
3. Adapt to the stressor. You can do so by reframing your thoughts and beliefs, looking at the problem from another perspective, learning to be okay with a "less than perfect" result, and practicing gratitude.
4. Accept the things that are beyond your power to change.

----
59 Help Guide, n.d.

Make time for fun

Let your happy inner child come out to play. Do fun, adventurous things and treat and pamper yourself, remembering that in doing so, you are also treating your inner child.

Manage your time well

Time management involves four main strategies:

- committing only to what you know you can accomplish
- prioritizing tasks
- breaking big goals into smaller ones and giving yourself reasonable (and, if necessary, flexible) deadlines for each goal
- delegating tasks to people you can trust

Overcome Your Own Resistance to Change

Sometimes the biggest obstacle standing in your way is your-self. To overcome your own resistance[60]:

- Take your journal and write down the precise benefits you will receive from making specific changes in your life.
- Embrace possible failure as an opportunity for growth.
- Know that failure is not guaranteed. Read about (and try to meet) people who have had similar challenges as you and who have overcome them.

----
60 Griggs, 2020.

3 CBT ACTIVITIES FOR REFRAMING THE CORE BELIEFS THAT HURT YOUR INNER CHILD

Core Beliefs

The following exercise shows how your core beliefs are like filters that lead you to see things in one way or another[61].

Let's take a situation in which you see a poster announcing auditions for a play in your local area. You have always loved acting and would love to try out.

> **The Situation:** There are auditions in the local area.
> **Negative Core Belief:** *I'm not good enough to get selected.*
> **Consequence:** I don't audition.
> **The Same Situation:** There are auditions in your area.
> **Positive Core Belief**: *I'm going to try out. The worst thing that can happen is that I don't get selected.*
> **Consequence:** I try out for the play.

Many people have negative core beliefs that harm their inner child. To begin challenging these beliefs, you must first recognize them.

Common negative beliefs include:

- *I'm not entertaining.*
- *I'm not interesting.*
- *I'm unlovable.*
- *I'm not a good friend/partner/person.*

---

61 Therapist Aid, n.d.

- *I'm not smart.*
- *I'm unattractive.*
- *I'm worthless.*
- *I'm undeserving.*

What is one of your negative core beliefs?

List three pieces of evidence that are contrary to your negative core belief.

Write down three situations in which your negative core belief caused you to refrain from participating in an activity or getting close to someone because you feared rejection.

✎…

✎…

✎…

✎…

Disrupting Irrational Beliefs

This exercise shows how beliefs can lead to thoughts, which can then influence your emotions and experiences. It also aims to help you differentiate between rational beliefs (those which are based on fact and which help achieve your goals and avoid conflicts) and irrational beliefs (negative interpretations of events that can cause you emotional pain or conflict)[62].

----
62 Schaffner, 2020.

Take your journal and write your answers to the following questions:

What is my belief? For example, *I am unlikable.*

Can I rationally back this belief? *I have fewer friends than other people, and I find it hard to start conversations and find interesting things to say.*

Are these ideas logically connected? *They are not necessarily connected because having many friends does not mean that all these relationships are high-quality.*

Who supports this belief, and what is their authority to do so? *My ex-girlfriend always said I was off-putting to others.*

What evidence shows that this belief is false? *The friends I do have call me regularly to meet up, and I am always welcome to call them or join them for their plans.*

What is the worst thing that could happen if I don't get the results I want? *I will continue to have a small group of friends.*

What good things can I make happen if I don't get the result I want? *I can work on getting closer to my friends and building great memories with them.*

✎...

✎...

✎...

✎...

Challenging Irrational Beliefs

This exercise encourages readers to challenge common irrational beliefs.

Common Irrational Beliefs:

- *If the person I am interested in doesn't love me back, I am worthless.*
- *I am only as good as my successes.*
- *It's not okay to be upset. I'm supposed to be happy and upbeat all the time.*
- *If ___ doesn't like me, then everyone else in the group must dislike me as well.*
- *Nothing will ever change.*
- *My life is so tough. It shouldn't be this unfair and meaningless.*
- *I shouldn't allow myself to be angry.*

Questions to Challenge These Beliefs

Think about each of the beliefs above and challenge them by asking the following questions:

- *What is the evidence for this idea?*
- *What is the evidence against this idea?*
- *Am I confusing my perception of things with fact?*
- *Am I using an "all or nothing" filter when I harbor this belief?*
- *Am I using exaggerated words like "always" or "never?"*
- *Am I making excuses to avoid taking action and making a change?*

---

63 Therapist Aid, n.d.

- *Am I interpreting something as a certainty when it could be a mere possibility or probability?*
- *Are my judgments based on my feelings instead of the available facts?*
- *Am I focusing on irrelevant factors?*

✎...

✎...

✎...

✎...

Challenging your negative core beliefs involves thinking about the past and how this affected your sense of self-worth. This can be challenging, but it is also infinitely rewarding. In the next chapter, we will move straight to Chapter 3: how to experiment with new behaviors and set healthy boundaries.

HELP OTHER ADULTS BUILD HEALTHY RELATIONSHIPS BY HEALING SOMEONE THEY HAVE LONG NEGLECTED—THEIR INNER CHILD

"Our brains are wired for connection, but trauma rewires them for protection. That's why healthy relationships are difficult for wounded people."

Earlier in this book, I mentioned that childhood trauma is far more common than you might ever imagine. In fact, the vast majority of people have experienced adverse childhood experiences. Many bury their hurt, thinking that rehashing old issues will only open old wounds.

But what happens when your wound never healed in the first place?

As adults, we are expected to put on a brave face and the current buzzword is undoubtedly mindfulness—or keeping your mind in the present moment.

That's all well and good, but until you heal, you cannot move forward. Study after study has shown that repressing emotions is linked to depression and other mental conditions. If you saw a child in pain on the road, would your instinct not be to run to them, embrace them, and offer protection?

Have you ever stopped to think why affording yourself the same kindness is sometimes so difficult?

In the first few chapters of this book, I highlighted the importance of dealing with past trauma. I explained that unresolved trauma leads you to choose attachment styles that may not be the healthiest, or the most conducive to a happy relationship.

You now know how traumatic experiences in childhood can affect your thoughts and core beliefs, and you know how important it is to reframe the distortions that lead you to behaviors that harm your relationships or keep you stuck in a rut.

If you feel that the techniques I shared are helping you see yourself and your life in a positive light, then let others know that they don't have to live in a constant state of hurt.

By leaving a review of this book on Amazon, you'll inspire other readers to know that healing their inner child begins by reframing your thoughts and beliefs to undo the pain that others have caused you.

Simply by letting other readers know how this book has helped you and what they'll find inside, you'll show them that they can make big changes in their outlook and happiness from day one.

Thank you so much for your help. By being open about how valuable inner child healing has been to you, you can help others find their child and welcome them with open arms.

6

STEP 3: EXPERIMENT WITH NEW BEHAVIORS

> "All life is an experiment. The more experiments you make the better."

— RALPH WALDO EMERSON

Hiding your vulnerability can result in stagnation or self-sabotage. If you find yourself putting up a front so that others don't reach the deepest, most vulnerable part of you, know that you could be missing out on some of the best things in life. These include the chance to meet new people that could vastly change the outcome of your professional and personal life for the better.

A 2021 study has shown that people often take part in self-sabotaging behaviors owing to three main factors:

- defensiveness
- difficulties trusting others
- a lack of relationship skills

Our behaviors can turn people on or off, and they can stop us from forming relationships. They can also propel us to move through relationships too quickly, deciding someone is right for us without getting to really know them. Self-sabotage can also cause us to stay in toxic relationships or remain in unhealthy ones that require us to work on key issues.

When you have a hurt inner child, you are more likely to engage in harmful behaviors because you are not used to trusting others or working on yourself in a productive, non-judgmental manner.

SINDRE

Sindre is a 30-something-year-old who moves from partner to partner. His exes have often called him a "serial monogamist." Although he doesn't like being alone, he doesn't seem to stick around beyond the initial "Velcro" stage of relationships. Sindre has very high standards, and when a potential partner doesn't comply with them fully, he quickly breaks things off. He only admits this to his closest friends—he fears trusting anyone fully. His excuse for breaking up with his partners is usually that he no longer feels the same way as in the beginning or that he realizes they aren't right for each other. When he breaks up with one person, he fondly recalls one of his exes and wonders if he didn't do the wrong thing by breaking up with them.

INSPIRATION FROM BRENÉ BROWN

If you are into TED talks, then one you can't miss out on is storyteller and vulnerability researcher Brené Brown's talk, *The Power of Vulnerability*. In this talk, she explains that when she was studying for her doctorate, she decided to delve into the subject of human connection. She found that the one thing that held people back from connecting with others was the feeling of shame. Many people go through life thinking that others will deem them unworthy if they discover some hidden secret about them[64].

Brown spent her next six years studying thousands of stories and conducting hours of long interviews. The vast amount of data she collected enabled her to divide people into two groups. One had a strong sense of worthiness, and the other comprised those who struggled to feel a sense of love and belonging. As she looked through story after story, she found that the one variable that separated people with a strong sense of belonging from those who lacked it was vulnerability. She states, "The definition of vulnerability is uncertainty, risk, and emotional exposure. But vulnerability is not weakness; it's our most accurate measure of courage[65]."

---

64 Brown, 2020.
65 Anne Silvers, n.d.

WHAT BEHAVIORS HURT YOUR INNER CHILD?

Your inner child may be hurting because of things beyond their control—for instance, a style of parenting that resulted in feelings of inadequacy or rejection. However, as an adult, you can continue to behave in a way that wounds your inner child further. Behaviors to watch out for include[66]:

Self-Criticism and Self-Blame

It can be easy to be hard on yourself in current times. The self-improvement monster, alongside a host of rules stipulated by influencers and media leaders, can lead you to compare yourself against unrealistic standards. As stated by model Cameron Russell, social media can be very misleading. She states that the images people see of models are a far cry from what they look like in real life. She says images are a work of art crafted by stylists, lighting experts, photographers, and editors[67]. Yet many young people compare themselves to unrealistic standards, and the result is a feeling of inadequacy.

Self-blame, meanwhile, comes from conditioning. It arises when, from a very early age, you are made to take on responsibility and ownership for things that you have not caused. If you were raised in a dysfunctional environment or you have experienced trauma, you can absorb pain deeply and end up blaming yourself for the hurt others cause you[68].

66 Brennan, 2021.
67 Lifestyle Desk, 2019.
68 Riverside Recovery, 2019.

Perfectionism

We spoke earlier about the strict rules you can set for yourself. Perfectionists lead their life according to a set of rigid rules. They feel a strong need to be or appear flawless, and when this need is maladaptive, it results in stress. The consequences of perfectionism are much deeper than mere disappointment. They include decreased productivity, increased vulnerability to anxiety, depression, anger, physical health issues, strained relationships, and an inability to give yourself fully to the present moment[69].

Ignoring or Suppressing Your Emotions

Emotional suppression happens when we push uncomfortable thoughts and feelings out of our minds. This habit can take many forms, including:

- overeating or excessively controlling their food intake
- escaping the pain through distractions like watching TV
- numbing pain through drugs or alcohol
- using sports or workouts to forget what is really going on inside.

We spoke earlier about mindfulness and how helpful it can be to accept your thoughts without allowing them to take over your mindset. Emotional regulation does not involve eliminating emotions but rather dealing with them productively—

69 Taylor, 2021.

even though it can be challenging to deal with emotions like sadness, anger, or shame.

Avoiding Triggers

Avoiding the situations and people that you know will upset you is smart, and it is an important way to avoid hurting your inner child. However, it is all a matter of degree. It is one thing, for instance, to avoid going to a party you know will be attended by an acquaintance who is always rude and condescending. It is quite another, however, to continuously miss out on social or work occasions because you don't like one person who will be going.

Avoidance can create more anxiety, and what's worse, it can lead to the breakdown of meaningful relationships in your life. It can also be stressful for others, who may tire of you setting rules for social occasions that they are not comfortable following.

If the thing or person that is stressing you out is an inevitable part of your life, then the positive move is to find a good way of coping with it.

In order to nip avoidance coping in the bud, try to identify your negative coping actions and make a plan to deal proactively with your sources of stress. For instance, if you don't like it when a colleague criticizes other workers to you, you won't gain much by trying to avoid them (after all, they are in your office, and you have to see them regularly). Instead, promise yourself that the next time you have a quiet moment with this colleague, you will say that you prefer not to talk about people who aren't present[70].

People-Pleasing

Helping others is an excellent quality, and it benefits the giver as much as the recipient. However, excessive people pleasing—doing more than you can or giving at the expense of your own health, happiness, and well-being—has various downsides. First, it negates your fundamental need for self-care. Second, it can result in passive aggression and resentment. Over time, it can feel like others are taking advantage of you. People pleasing also interferes with your ability to enjoy the time you spend with others in a relaxed state. Finally, it can lead to stress and depression[71].

Overworking

Working too many hours is one of the biggest contributors to factors such as obesity, type 2 diabetes, heart disease, stress, anxiety, and depression. You were not made to be sitting at a desk for hours on end. Indeed, one study showed that working for more than 61 hours per week increases the risk of having high blood pressure. In a given year, over 745,000 people die from work-related stroke or heart disease. Being overworked is no laughing matter, and if this issue affects you, you have two choices: stay where you are and reduce your hours, or find a new job. No workplace is worth shortening your lifespan over[72].

----

70 Scott, 2022.
71 James Madison University, n.d.
72 Wooll, 2022.

HOW CAN YOU CHANGE THE BEHAVIORS THAT HURT YOUR INNER CHILD?

Changing the behaviors that change your inner child involves five strategies. You don't have to tackle them all at once, but eventually, all these strategies can build a foolproof shield for your inner child.

1. Setting Boundaries

We all have boundaries—the unwritten rules through which we let ourselves and others know what is acceptable and what is not. For instance, you may have specific boundaries with your children, such as "I do not talk about issues with people who are shouting at me." A boundary with friends may be, "I cannot receive calls during work hours," and a boundary with a partner might be, "I enjoy receiving texts from you, but not every hour."

Boundaries are all about you. They involve your choices, limits, and behavior. Boundaries do not cut people out. They invite the right ones in[73].

Healthy boundaries sound something like this:

- "I am affectionate, but I prefer to avoid public displays of affection.
- "I need my personal body space to be respected."
- "I prefer shaking hands to hugging."
- "I prefer not to share that information."
- "I cannot do that right now."
- "I do not do that."

----
73 Weinstock, 2023.

Boundaries can be healthy or unhealthy, depending upon whether they are[74]:

1. **Clear:** These are healthy boundaries. They are unequivocal and flexible. In healthy relationships and families, individuals are close, but they are also free to say what they are okay with.
2. **Rigid:** These boundaries are closed and inflexible. There is less engagement between family members or spouses, and it can be hard for them to express their individuality or express their wants and needs.
3. **Open:** They can be loose or difficult to express. Families and relationships with open boundaries can find it hard to have their wants and needs met. People can become enmeshed and display codependent behaviors.

When health boundaries exist, you confidently:

- Say no when you are uncomfortable doing something.
- Clearly communicate your boundaries, wants, and needs.
- Respect others' wants and needs.
- Respect others' values, ideas, and opinions.
- Feel free to share personal information because you trust others.
- Adapt boundaries as required without compromising them in a way that ends up hurting your inner child.

74 Brooten-Brooks, 2022.

Six Types of Boundaries

There are many areas of your life that require boundary setting. Boundaries can be:

Physical: These boundaries include your personal space and bodily autonomy.

Examples of physical boundary violations:

- standing too close to someone
- hugging someone or touching them when this action is unwelcome
- touching someone's body in a way that they are uncomfortable with

Useful phrases for setting physical boundaries:

- "I don't like hugging/kissing/hand-shaking."
- "I've asked you not to pull my hair. It makes me feel uncomfortable."
- "I don't like being tickled."
- "Could you move back a little?"

Sexual: These are related to your sexuality and your intimate space.

Examples of sexual boundary violations:

- someone insisting on a practice or activity you are not comfortable with

- someone insisting on sexual activity when you are not interested
- someone touching you intimately when you don't want them to

Useful phrases for setting sexual boundaries:

- "I don't feel comfortable doing____."
- "I asked you not to touch me."
- "I am not okay with that."

Intellectual: These establish respect for your thoughts, ideas, and opinions.

Examples of intellectual boundary violations:

- someone telling you your idea is stupid
- someone laughing at an idea
- someone not listening to you or not taking your point of view seriously

Useful phrases for setting intellectual boundaries:

- "That is my opinion, and all our opinions matter."
- "I explained that I find it hurtful when you laugh at my ideas."
- "I don't agree with you on that point."

Emotional: These are boundaries you set to protect your feelings or personal information.

Examples of emotional boundary violations:

- someone telling others a secret you asked them not to share
- someone insisting you have no reason to cry
- someone belittling an emotion you have shared with them

Useful phrases for setting emotional boundaries:

- "My emotions are valid, and I expect them to be respected."
- "I am not okay with my personal information being shared."
- "When I ask someone to keep a secret, it is hurtful when they disrespect my wishes and tell others about it."

Material: These boundaries protect your financial resources and things.

Examples of material boundary violations:

- someone taking your credit card and making a purchase without your permission
- someone expecting you to pay for everything when you go out
- someone who takes or borrows your things (for instance, your clothing or a book) without asking

Useful phrases for setting material boundaries:

- "I don't share my credit card information with anyone."
- "I don't share that item of clothing because it is delicate."
- "Let's each pay our own dish today."

Time: Includes how you wish to spend your time.

Examples of time boundary violations:

- showing up late continuously
- constantly interrupting you when you are busy on a task
- demanding that you spend time with them that you just don't have

Useful phrases for setting time boundaries:

- "I show up on time and expect others to do so."
- "I cannot spend time with you when I have to complete a work task."
- "I don't have more than one hour to spend on lunch."

How to Set Healthy Boundaries

Setting healthy boundaries requires the same strategies, regardless of the specifics involved. These strategies include:

1. Identify your goal. What do you want to achieve by setting this boundary?

2. Start small. Practice with small boundaries before getting to more challenging ones.

3. Say what you want and need clearly.

4. Practice boundary setting with the people you come across daily.

5. Focus on the larger picture instead of on tiny details.

6. Use "I don't" frequently. Avoid using phrases like "I can't, because…" or you could end up wasting too much time and energy explaining yourself. Your boundaries are there because you decided to set them.

7. Say no when you need to, and don't feel the need to explain why.

8. Be consistent, and don't give in. You are the only guardian of your boundaries, so don't let yourself down.

9. Make time for yourself. It will enable you to think about your current boundaries and consider whether you need to set a new one.

10. Know you can add your own boundaries within a setting that already has specific norms (for instance, you can set your own limits at work).

2. Facing Your Emotions

When you are feeling upset, take time to pause before your mind starts racing, and you begin to feel helpless, hurt, or fearful[75].

----

75 Mental Health America, n.d.

1. Take a pause. If possible, head to a green area, which will calm you down. Breathe and bring your mind back to the present moment.
2. Define your emotion. Try to work out if you are feeling angry, sad, disgusted, surprised, fearful, trusting, or joyful or if you are anticipating something.
3. Think about a practical step you can take to make yourself feel better.
4. Help yourself by doing one of the following activities:

- Take part in an activity that lifts your mood.
- Express your feelings (for instance, by punching a pillow, crying, or making a gratitude list.
- Brainstorm solutions to your problem and commit to the solution you think is best. If the solution doesn't work, you can try another one.
- Doing something for someone in need.
- Taking up a stress-relieving hobby.
- Do something that lowers your stress levels—including meditation, breathing, and going for a walk outdoors.

3. Exposing Yourself to Challenging Situations

One of the best ways to "beat" the situations that cause you stress or tension is to take challenging situations by the horns instead of shying away from them. Get out of your comfort zone to try something new. For instance, if you have always wanted to learn to scuba dive, bake macarons, or mountain bike, what's stopping you? A few ideas that may inspire you include[76]:

----
76 Wooll, 2022.

1. Find new ways to prioritize your mental health.
2. Limit the time you spend on the Internet and social media.
3. Write daily in your journal.
4. Organize your wardrobe or garage and have a garage sale or give unwanted items away.
5. Improve your memory by taking up a creative hobby.
6. Sign up for a class or group exercise session.
7. Accept a challenging task at work.
8. Join a networking group.
9. Go for a half-hour walk daily.

4. Committing to a Positive Work-Life Balance

Be firm about the number of hours you work, and avoid checking your email or work phone after hours. If you allow work to overtake your entire day, you will open up the doors to emotional exhaustion, a feeling of detachment from others or the world around you, and reduced productivity and motivation.

5. Experimenting With New Behaviors

If a specific behavior leads you nowhere, why persist in displaying it? In past chapters, we have seen how CBT encourages you to change your thoughts and beliefs. However, a core component of this therapy involves trying out new behaviors. Doing so can have a surprising and dramatically positive effect on your thoughts and emotions.

3 EXERCISES TO CHANGE THE BEHAVIORS THAT HURT YOUR INNER CHILD

Testing Your Thought With a Behavior

This exercise encourages you to try new behaviors and see how they change the way you think or feel about a situation.

Take your journal and write down one belief or rule you want to test.

For instance: *Nobody at work likes me.*

Indicate an alternative belief.

Various co-workers like me.

Rate your initial belief: How strong is it from one to ten (with ten being the strongest and one the weakest)?

Answer: *8*

Write down one behavior you will use to challenge it.

I will ask a couple of colleagues to lunch today.

What do you think will happen?

I think they will say they're busy.

How sure are you that this will happen?

They don't spend much time talking to me.

Indicate the safety behaviors you will avoid during the experiment.

I will avoid asking them by text. I will go directly to their desks and ask them.

List down the evidence you will use to assess which belief is more likely to be true.

If they say yes, or they say they are busy but make a lunch plan for me another day, it's a good indication that they would like to get to know me better.

Carry out the experiment and write down what happened.

I asked Bill and Amir to lunch, and Bill was busy but said he was sad he couldn't go. He had a meeting but said he would go next time. Amir and I had pizza and enjoyed a good laugh.

Rate your initial belief again.

Answer: *4*

Rate how correct your prediction was from one to ten.

Answer: *2*

Ask yourself what you can conclude from this experiment.

> *People probably want to get to know me as much as I want to get to know them. I just need to suggest more plans.*

List down new experiments this one can inspire.

> *I'm going to suggest a beach day to everyone next week.*

✎...

✎...

✎...

✎...

Expose Yourself to Challenging Situations

This experiment is similar to that used to curb phobias. It involves facing fear and other unpleasant emotions and sensations to discover that they are usually not as powerful as you imagined[77].

Engage in the behaviors that you fear will cause you emotions like fear, embarrassment, or sadness. Use the process in Exercise 1 to do so, but try to do exactly what you typically avoid doing. You might:

----

77 Morin, 2020.

- Ask someone on a date you "know" will say no.
- Go to karaoke and sing a heavy metal song, even if you have terrible stage fright.
- Go out on Saturday and Sunday (if you usually stay in because you feel going out is a waste of time).
- Go to work when you feel anxious or depressed instead of staying home.
- Go up to someone you like and introduce yourself.
- If you're an introvert, pretend you are an extrovert for a day and go up to various people at work or a party.

✎...

✎...

✎...

✎...

Complete this Exposure Worksheet

This exercise is similar to 1., but it also involves deciding on how you will reward yourself[78]. Take your journal and:

- Write down one fear.
- Decide how you will face this fear.
- Predict what you think will happen.
- Predict how high your anxiety will be during the experiment. (Use a one to ten rating scale, with ten being the highest anxiety and one the lowest.)

---

78 Washington University, n.d.

- Decide on a reward you will give yourself for going through with the experiment.
- Once you finish the experiment, write down how the experience compared to what you predicted.
- Did anything surprise you?
- What did you learn?
- What evidence do you have that you can handle situations that you fear?
- How high did your anxiety actually get?

✎…

✎…

✎…

✎…

You have now aced the fundamentals of CBT, having discovered how to reframe your thoughts and beliefs and try out new behaviors. Step 4 is just as vital. It involves building your emotional intelligence.

7

STEP 4: BUILD YOUR EMOTIONAL INTELLIGENCE

 "Emotions can get in the way or get you on the way."

— MAVIS MAZHURA

E motional intelligence accounts for nearly 90 percent of what sets high performers apart from peers with similar technical skills and knowledge. Only about 36 percent of people in the world are emotionally Intelligent, according to research undertaken by author Travis Bradbury[79]. These people may work to hone their "hard skills" (such as their training and education), ignoring the importance of skills such as self-awareness, active listening, and empathy.

Companies are increasingly seeking to recruit people with "soft skills" such as teamwork, goal orientation, and the ability to resolve conflicts with others with a view to moving forward. Emotional intelligence is also a priceless tool in your relation-

79 Cornerstone University, 2017.

ships, as it enables you to communicate well, assert your needs, and help others feel understood and cared for as well.

FORREST

If you are a film fan, then you may recall the award-winning film *Forrest Gump*, about a man (Forrest) with physical and mental disabilities who does not let these issues stand in the way of his relationships. This character exemplifies the essence of emotional intelligence; he is impossible not to like. For one, Forest shares his vulnerability with others and is open about his life experiences, as well as his thoughts and beliefs. He also shows that he is an empathetic listener and a team player—to the point that he risks his life various times to save the soldiers in his platoon. In one of the most emotive scenes (when his best friend, Bubba, dies in his arms on the battlefield), Forrest displays his usual honesty when Bubba asks, "Why did this happen?" Forrest answers: "You got shot." Later, he muses that if he had known this was the last time he'd speak to Bubba, he would have said something more meaningful.

Forrest's actions throughout the film display a kind of interpersonal intelligence that most human beings can only aspire to. Loyalty, transparency, trustworthiness, and teamwork are just some of the skills he displays. Many would say Forest is innately wise, but throughout the film, we get glimpses into his childhood and understand that his soulful mother had plenty to do with the kind and childlike way he viewed life.

WHAT IS EMOTIONAL INTELLIGENCE?

Emotional intelligence is the ability to perceive, evaluate, express, and control emotions, as stated by Mayer et al[80].

The signs of emotional intelligence include:

- an ability to identify and describe your (and others') emotions
- self-confidence and self-acceptance
- knowing your strengths and weaknesses
- having a growth mentality
- being flexible to change
- being empathetic
- being sensitive to others' problems
- taking responsibility for your mistakes
- knowing how to control your emotions in difficult situations
- being a good listener

HOW EMOTIONAL INTELLIGENCE RELATES TO INNER CHILD HEALING

Building your emotional intelligence can help you be more aware of the relationship between your triggers and behaviors. It can help you know when your inner child will likely "act up." By knowing your own strengths and weaknesses and the specific vulnerabilities of your inner child, you can take control of thoughts and emotions that harm you and the relationships you value.

----

80 Cherry, 2023.

THE COMPONENTS OF EMOTIONAL INTELLIGENCE

There are four components of emotional intelligence[81]:

1. **Self-Awareness** is the ability to identify and understand your emotions and your effect on others. This is the very foundation of emotional intelligence. Knowing your triggers, strengths, and weaknesses and being able to identify the link between your emotions and behaviors is vital if you are to manage your emotions better.
2. **Self-Regulation** refers to your ability to control your emotions. It includes skills like self-soothing, impulse control, and staying positive even when the going gets tough.
3. **Social Awareness** refers to your ability to understand others' emotions, to understand that people don't necessarily think or feel about things the same way you do.
4. **Social Skills** like influence, teamwork, and conflict resolution are all vital social skills that help you build healthy relationships with others.

Take a look at this table, which shows a few examples that highlight what having a high emotional intelligence quotient (EQ) compares to having a low quotient.

81 Harvard Professional Development, n.d.

HIGH EQ	LOW EQ
Says what they want and need	Has trouble expressing their wants and needs assertively.
Keeps their cool during stressful situations	Blows a fuse/has difficulty controlling their anger frequently
Understands the link between how they think and feel, and their behaviors	Feels overwhelmed by their emotions
Influences and inspires others to achieve common goals	Has little influence over others

BUILDING YOUR EMOTIONAL INTELLIGENCE TO HEAL YOUR INNER CHILD

The following strategies will make you a better companion to your inner child while also helping you interact fruitfully with others.

Think before you react.

When something triggers or provokes you, distance yourself from the situation and be aware of your thoughts and emotions. Be careful not to behave impulsively, or you could regret it later.

Build your self-awareness.

To build your self-awareness, take the following steps:

1. Complete the SWOT (Strengths, Weaknesses, Opportunities, Threats) Analysis worksheet. (Exercise 1, below)
2. Use your journal to reflect on the day's most important events. Write down the thoughts and emotions

surrounding your event and how you responded to them. Doing so will enable you to identify what works best and what you can improve.

3. Make time for daily mindfulness meditation. Doing so will enable you to acknowledge uncomfortable or painful thoughts and emotions while obtaining a healthy distance from them.

4. Be empathetic, especially when situations are most stressful. Don't be tempted to fly off the handle at someone, even if they may provoke you. Think about the longstanding damage that words can do. If you have to, take a break from the other person. Don't dump your negative thoughts and emotions onto them or use tactics such as blame, judgment, or shame.

5. Ask the people you love for feedback. Approach those you know are honest enough not to tell you what you need to hear.

THE VALUE OF A 360° ASSESSMENT

If you are a manager, business owner, or executive, conduct a 360° assessment[82]. This professional assessment system involves asking your employees to fill out an anonymous online form that asks questions covering a wide array of workplace compe-tencies. It comprises questions that are measured on a visible scale and leaves room for written comments.

This assessment allows managers and leaders to get completely honest feedback and to understand how others perceive them. It takes guts and strength to conduct one of these, and you may

---

82 Custom Insight, n.d.

be surprised to find areas for improvement in your management style that you would never have otherwise identified. Truth is power, and receiving honest feedback about your strengths and weaknesses is no less than a gift for any leader.

360º assessments cover competencies like leadership, communication, collaboration, problem-solving, adaptability, initiative, emotional intelligence, customer focus, strategic thinking, performance management, integrity, innovation, and more.

- Know why you do the things you do. Knowing your strengths and weaknesses isn't enough. It is also important to look back at your life and think about why you may be better at some aspects of emotional intelligence than others. Remember that emotional intelligence is not made up of a static set of skills. You can work on areas you and others have defined as a weakness, but you should know why you are prone to thoughts or behaviors that stand in the way of your progress.
- Have empathy for others. Even during times when others get on your nerves, try to see things from their perspective. Why do you think they are displaying behaviors you don't like, and how can you let them know without making them feel rejected or defensive?
- Accept criticism and responsibility. One of the strongest marks of a good friend, colleague, and partner is the ability to take negative feedback non-defensively. The buck doesn't stop there, however. Apologizing is important as it displays that you are committed to

avoiding the words and behaviors that hurt someone else. When you apologize, make sure you back your words with actions. Doing so will mark you as a trustworthy person, one with integrity.

- Move on after you make a mistake. We mentioned how overthinking your errors can hurt your inner child, who may already be struggling with self-esteem issues. By all means, analyze your thought and behavioral patterns, but once you reframe your thoughts or decide to try out a new behavior, let it go and move to something else. Remember that your inner child has nowhere to escape when your inner critic commences its onslaught.

- Say no when you need to. Don't be so determined to please everyone else that you give more than you can or overwork to prove your worth. In Chapter Six, we mentioned how damaging people-pleasing can be. Set clear boundaries with others, and don't give in to others' attempts at overstepping them. Remember that if you do so, some people will walk all over your inner child.

- Share your feelings with others. Remember how important it is to open up and lose the fear of being vulnerable. People feel more connected to "real" people —those with trials and mishaps that are similar to their own. Of course, to preserve your inner child, confide very private or intimate matters only with people who are trustworthy.

- Hone your listening skills. Work on your active listening skills by giving others the time they need to talk and by being truly interested in what they have to say. Show you are interested in what they are telling you by using open, warm body language. Look them in the eyes as they are speaking, and keep your hands by your side (not crossed over your chest). Nod once in a while to show you're listening to them, and say things like, "Yes, I understand," or "That must be very difficult/challenging/painful for you," and similar.

- Don't judge others. As much as you think you know your friends and loved ones, everyone has an inner child who may keep pain and rejection to themselves. Many people have undergone traumatic experiences but do not feel comfortable sharing this trauma. Significant people in your life may eventually open up to you, but until they do, be careful of the words you use and the judgments you make.

- Embrace opportunities to work collaboratively. Group projects enable you to sharpen a host of vital emotional intelligence skills. When you are working alongside others, be actively participative, communicate effectively, and show your ability to compromise and come to a consensus.

- Work on cultural sensitivity and an appreciation for diversity. Find ways to expose yourself to different cultures, backgrounds, and perspectives[83]. Be respectful in your actions and, if you are a manager or business owner, invest time and resources in introducing inclusion efforts and diversity initiatives to your organization. Make sure your executive team comprises a diverse range of people. Honor multiple religions and

----
83 Firstup, n.d.

cultural practices in your workplace, and encourage open dialogue about matters such as gender pay inequality. Strengthen anti-discrimination policies and give due priority to creating a multigenerational, multilingual team.

3 CBT EXERCISES TO BUILD EMOTIONAL INTELLIGENCE:

Write a Letter to Your Inner Child

Writing your inner child a letter helps you feel more connected to them. You may find the following template useful, but your letter should be personal and bespoke:

Dear___(your own name),
I know you want___
I know you need___
I know you feel hurt because___
I can take steps to end your pain by___
You are safe now. I am here with you, and I am constantly learning new tools to protect you.
Forgive me for not learning these tools sooner.
I know I may have silenced you in the past, but I am here now.
I want you to express your pain, hurt, and anger freely.
You don't need to hide because of me.
Come out into the light. You will find an unconditional friend in me.

I see you. I hear you. I feel you. I love you.

✎…

✎…

✎…

✎…

Emotional Fact-Checking

This exercise can help you manage your emotions more effectively.

Take your journal and ask the following questions[84].

1. What event triggered my emotion?
2. What assumptions am I making about what occurred?
3. Do my emotions and their intensity match the objective facts of the situation? Or am I simply matching my assumptions to the situation?

✎…

✎…

✎…

✎…

----
84 Therapist Aid, n.d.

Discover Your Personal Iceberg

The Personal Iceberg is a technique that is used to explore oneself. It looks something like this[85]:

At the tip of the iceberg (the only part of it that is visible to everyone) is your behavior. Beneath the water, in successive layers, are your thoughts, emotions, expectations, values, yearnings, and self.

Take your journal and write something next to each layer when a challenging situation arises. An example is given below:

The Situation: Your husband is annoyed with you, and you frequently argue over the amount of time you spend on social media.

Thought: Your thoughts are the intellectual activity that involves your subjective consciousness.

Example: *He's so controlling! He is trying to stop me from spending my free time the way I want to!*

Emotions: Your emotions occur as a result of your thoughts. Emotions can sometimes be hard to define because you can have various feelings at once.

I feel controlled, belittled, and judged. I feel angry and frustrated.

Expectations: Your expectations are built from the collection of thoughts, emotions, and behaviors you have been exposed to

---

85 Lavelda Naylor, n.d.

for many years. They can be based on childhood experiences, legends, the media, your culture, and more.

> *I expect to be judged because he often judges the way I enjoy spending my free time or the type of media that I consume. I expect him to berate me when I'm online because he always does. Therefore, I say I'm working when I'm actually chatting with someone on Twitter.*

Values: These are the ideas that form the foundation of our lives. We hold them dearly and aim to act in accordance with them.

> *I value being honest about what I'm doing. I value my freedom to spend my free time as I want. I value accepting others and their tastes.*

Yearnings: These are our wants, needs, wishes, and hopes.

> *I work hard and need to unwind when I get home. I love connecting with my friends from back home. I wish my husband had as much fun as I do sharing ideas and opinions on social media.*

Self: This is who we were, are, and will be. The self is not fixed, but it does represent the entirety of who you are from the time you are born until the time you die. The way you see yourself has a powerful effect on your inner child. If you have low self-esteem, for instance, then your inner child may find it hard to stick up for themselves or pursue their wants and needs.

Many people in my life have tried to control me. It has made me fiercely protective of my independence and reluctant to explain why I do the things I do.

✎...

✎...

✎...

✎...

With the knowledge you have obtained from this exercise, you can sit down with your husband during a calm movement and say something like:

"When you criticize me for spending time on social media, it makes me feel controlled. I want you to know that what seems like a waste of time to you is something that gives me great joy. It enables me to connect with my childhood friends and feel understood. Having a laugh with them calms the stress I build during the day. When I was a child, I was not allowed to do all the things I wanted. For instance, at an age when my peers were all going out and having meet-ups, I was not allowed to attend. This is why now, I value taking the time I need to connect with my friends. What about you? Did you have a lot of freedom as a child?"

The iceberg method can be very enlightening if you work your way through all the layers and reach the self. It can help you communicate with others thoughtfully instead of impulsively.

In this chapter, you have worked on building your emotional intelligence. Sometimes, however, certain situations and people can really put your patience to the test. Read on to discover how to overcome your inner child's strongest enemies.

8

STEP 5: OVERCOME YOUR INNER CHILD'S ENEMIES

> *"There are certain emotions that will kill your drive; frustration and confusion. You can change these to a positive force. Frustration means you are on the verge of a breakthrough. Confusion can mean you are about to learn something. Expect the breakthrough and expect to learn."*

— KATHLEEN SPIKE

Triggers are stimuli that stimulate your fight or flight response—the physiological reaction that happens when you are faced with something mentally or physically terrifying. It kicks off when specific hormones are released that prepare your body to either face your aggressor or flee to safety[86].

----

86 Cherry, 2022.

LIBBY

Libby (not her real name) is a friend in her early 40s working on healing her inner child. We recently had a cup of coffee, and she explained how fascinated she was to discover that she often used cognitive distortions or filters to make sense of the world around her. Inner child healing helped her see how often she assumed that a friend or neighbor had done or said something with bad intentions. By using facts to make her decisions instead of biased thoughts, she built solid friendships with the people that surrounded her and told me she had never felt so supported.

FIGHT OR FLIGHT

While triggers vary greatly from person to person, one thing they all have in common is the response: hyper-arousal, intrusive reliving of the event, dissociation, numbing, angry outbursts, reckless behavior, self-harm, an exaggerated startle response, hypervigilance, concentration problems, and sleep disturbance[87].

Triggers can lead you to think you are in life-threatening danger when this is far from the truth. Their effects can be so overpowering, however, that you can feel frozen in place. The fight or flight response can set off a panic attack, which is one of the most challenging effects of anxiety disorder.

----

87 Laguardia & Michalsen, 2017.

The fight of flight response has three stages[88]:

Stage 1: The Alarm Stage

This is when your central nervous system goes into overdrive, preparing your body to react to your aggressor. Once your brain knows it is under stress, it activates the release of adrenalin. Your heart starts beating faster, you begin to take in shorter, more frequent breaths, and your blood pressure rises. Oxygen and sugar are shunted into your bloodstream, so your body can respond if injury or disaster should strike. Your body prioritizes blood flow to the parts of your body you need to take action and shuts processes like digestion.

Stage 2: The Resistance Stage

After the threat in Stage 1 has passed, your body attempts to recover and regulate your heart rate, blood pressure, and breathing rate. However, you are still alert and ready for action should the threat return. Eventually, your body returns to its normal, relaxed state.

When you are under chronic stress, your body may never get the chance to recover completely. This can lead to anxiety and Stage 3 of the fight or flight response.

Stage 3: Exhaustion

When your body cannot recover from stress, it becomes depleted, harming your immunity and other systems. Chronic

----
88 Hyland, 2022.

stress is linked to a host of serious diseases and conditions, including heart disease, diabetes, digestive issues, depression, and anxiety. It can be one of your inner child's worst enemies.

How Can You Keep the Fight or Flight Response at Bay?

You have an important role in stopping chronic stress from harming your health and leading to mental anguish. The techniques to tame the fight or flight response are, interestingly, the same ones you need to respect, love, and care for your inner child. They include consuming a healthy diet that is rich in fruits and vegetables, exercising, breathing, using positive self-talk, seeing friends, and getting professional help if you need it. The CBT exercises contained throughout this book will also stop stress from causing everyday issues such as headaches, upset tummy, and difficulties falling asleep.

TRAUMA TRIGGERS AND YOUR INNER CHILD

Triggers in your daily life can trigger memories and thoughts that bring your inner child to the fore. They can make the inner child feel helpless, panicky, unsafe, stressed, and overwhelmed.

Your inner child can react with fear, panic, agitation, or anger. You may also experience flashbacks, which make it very hard to keep your mind in a relaxed state.

COMMON TRIGGERS THAT BRING YOUR INNER CHILD TO THE FORE

Some of your inner child's strongest triggers can include:

- anger that arises from unmet needs
- a feeling that someone is rejecting or abandoning you
- feeling insecure
- vulnerability
- anxiety
- shame
- guilt

HOW TO DEAL WITH TRAUMA TRIGGERS

Triggers are impossible to avoid, so it is vital to devise and utilize a strategy when they hit. The following four-step approach can stop triggers from taking over your happiness and wellbeing[89].

1. Focus on what is happening around you in the present moment.
2. Remind yourself that your thoughts and emotions are a logical response to trauma.
3. Perform controlled breathing exercises.
4. Use the flashback halting protocol to stop trauma from bringing you down or setting off the stress response. This involves reading and answering the following questions:

----
89 Wright, 2021.

- *Right now, I am feeling___(angry/scared/frightened, etc.).*
- *My body is responding by___(trembling/sweating/muscle tightening/a rapid heart rate, etc.) because I recall___(a person or situation that caused you distress).*
- *Yet, it is now___(say the current date and time).*
- *And I am here at___(say where you are).*
- *And I can see___(list or name five things you can see right now).*
- *And so I know that___(the traumatic event) is not happening now.*

STRENGTHENING YOUR SELF-CONCEPT

Building a strong self-concept can also help lessen the effects that difficult circumstances and people cause you.

WHAT IS THE SELF-CONCEPT?

The self-concept plays a key role in social and humanistic psychology. Lewis (1990) suggests that the development of self-concept has two aspects[90]:

- **The Existential Self:** This is the most basic part of the self-concept. It arises when a child first realizes that they are a separate entity from others.
- **The Categorical Self:** The categorical self comes to the fore when the child realizes that they are aware that they are an object in the world. In other words, they have properties such as tall/small. This self can be categorized according to age, skill, size, gender, etc.

----

90 Department of Educational Psychology SNDT Women's University, n.d.

Carl Rogers (1959), on the other hand, espoused that the self-concept comprises three components[91]:

- **Your Self-Image:** This is the way you see yourself—this does not have to reflect reality. For instance, you may see yourself as tall, but others may perceive you as of average height.
- **Your Self-Esteem:** This encompasses the extent to which you value yourself. Self-esteem is based on four key factors: how others react to you, how you compare yourself to others, your social roles (for instance, being a doctor is linked to high self-esteem, while being a prisoner is linked to low self-esteem), and identification (the extent to which you identify with your social role.
- **Your Ideal Self:** This is what someone you would like to be. If there is a big gap between who you think you are and your ideal self, then your self-esteem can suffer.

EXAMPLES OF SELF-CONCEPT

Below are a few examples of the messages you give yourself. These messages depend on your self-concept:

- *I see myself as intelligent.*
- *I perceive myself as an important member of my community.*
- *I see myself as a good friend.*
- *I see myself as caring.*
- *I am a poor time manager.*
- *I am unpopular.*
- *I am good at drawing.*

----
91 Online Learning College, 2022.

- *I am weak.*

CONGRUENCE AND INCONGRUENCE

When children are treated with love and care, their self-concept is aligned with reality (it is congruent). On the other hand, when their needs are not met, they can have an incongruent self-concept. We mentioned before that one of the main goals of CBT is to help you see things as they are, based on evidence. A poor sense of self can sadly lead you to think the worst of yourself or to make a situation worse than it actually is because you would rather "give up now" than have hope and be let down.

People with a poor sense of self often use cognitive distortions or filters to make the world a more predictable place. Sadly, these filters can cause you to misinterpret intentions and interpret opinions as fact.

BOOSTING YOUR SELF-CONCEPT

To help your inner child see themselves as more confident and worthy of a great life, embrace the following strategies[92]:

1. Find supportive people, mentors, and leaders who bring out the best in you.
2. Share your insecurities, and don't be afraid to show your vulnerability.
3. Read stories that inspire you.
4. Be self-compassionate.

----

92 Cherry, 2022.

5. Quiet your inner critic if they bring you down instead of helping you work on key areas in your life.
6. Notice the positive things around you.

Self-Concept Questionnaire by Dr. Saraswat

If you are keen to measure your self-concept, then answering the renowned self-concept questionnaire by Dr. Raj Kumar Saraswat will provide you with helpful answers. This questionnaire features 48 items and can be accessed online. Scribd allows you to access it by subscribing to this site with a 30-day free trial or by uploading a document of your own. The questionnaire can be accessed at: https://www.scribd.com/document/296465065/1-Self-Concept

HABIT LOOPS

Another big enemy of your inner child is unhelpful habit loops. Habit loops were first described by journalist Charles Duhigg[93]. He argued that habit loops have three main components:

The Cue: This is the trigger that starts the habitual behavior. This trigger can be:

- a specific place
- a specific time
- specific people
- your last action
- the way you feel in a given moment

---

93 Raypole, 2021.

The Routine: This is the behavior you repeat when your trigger arises. For instance:

- When you feel stressed, you might feel like having a drink.
- When you are bored, you might log onto Instagram and start watching stories.
- When you are nervous, you might start snacking.

The Reward: This is the result of the behavior you display. Rewards can be positive (if they reaffirm helpful routines) or negative (if they reinforce habits you don't want). For instance, if you have a habit of turning the light off and going to bed at 10 pm every night, then this can help you ensure a good night's sleep.

However, if every time you are anxious at night, you snack on unhealthy foods, you could end up putting on weight or feeling uncomfortable. This, in turn, could interfere with your sleep quality.

To break the habit loop, you need to:

1. Identify the routine.
2. Try alternative rewards.
3. Explore your triggers. (discuss location, time, emotional state, people around you, and your last action.)
4. Find a way around those cues.

4 EXERCISES TO COMBAT YOUR INNER CHILD'S ENEMIES

Designing a collage

Create a collage that represents who you are[94]. You can use pictures, words, and symbols. Cut pictures from a magazine, print online images, or draw the items yourself.

Focus on the things that give your life meaning. Keep this collage handy so you can remind yourself that the key to healing your inner child lies in pursuing these ideas, thoughts, and activities.

Five Traits

This exercise seeks to help you define your strengths and weaknesses and to stick to the traits that make you happy[95].

Write down five traits that define you. For each trait, ask yourself:

- Do you like this trait?
- Do you want to keep it?
- If you gave this trait up, what impact would it have on your life?
- If you gave up two more traits, what kind of person would it make you?

----

94 Ackerman, 2018.
95 Ackerman, 2018.

✎...

✎...

✎...

✎...

This Is Me

This exercise aims to help you understand yourself better. Take your journal and write your answers to the following questions[96]:

- I feel successful when___.
- My favorite pastime is___.
- I wish I could___.
- If I could make three wishes come true, they would be___.
- I feel depressed when___.
- A trait I would like to improve is___.
- I excel at___.
- My family is___.
- The most important thing to me is___.
- The thing I love most about myself is___.

✎...

✎...

✎...

✎...

---

96 Utah Education Network, n.d.

Classical Conditioning Worksheet

This exercise helps you understand how to break bad habits by choosing a conditioned (learned) response to your triggers instead of allowing unconditioned responses (natural responses you have no control of) to lead to unhelpful habits[97].

Take your journal and ask yourself the following questions:

1. What is the current habit I would like to change? Example: Snacking at night when I'm stressed.
2. What triggers my habit? Thinking about my breakup.
3. What unconditioned, natural response do I have to this trigger? Reaching for food.
4. What conditioned (learned) response can I employ when this trigger arises? Engage in a mindful activity such as breathing.
5. What are my thoughts about the trigger? I think my partner did not respect me, and I am angry at myself for confiding in them.
6. What is the current reward I give myself for my habit? Food.
7. Why do I wish to change this habit? I am feeling sluggish.
8. What is my motivation for wanting to change it? I want to feel energized, and I don't want to have sugar cravings.
9. What healthy or positive habit can I replace my negative habit with? Mindfulness meditation.

----
97 Virginia Counseling, n.d.

10. What tools will help me implement the new habit? My essential oil diffuser, calming music, and a soft and comfy chair.

✎...

✎...

✎...

✎...

You now know the five steps to healing your inner child. However, if you enjoy trying out different methods, I have provided a bonus chapter where you will find two approaches that are gaining ground when it comes to inner child healing: NLP and Acceptance and Commitment Therapy.

9

BONUS CHAPTER: NLP AND ACT
FOR INNER CHILD HEALING

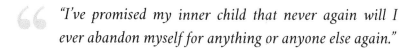

"I've promised my inner child that never again will I ever abandon myself for anything or anyone else again."

— WYNONNA JUDD

S uccessful author, Tony Robbins, uses an NLP technique called Incantations every day. Incantations differ from affirmations in that incantations focus on changing your physiology[98]. To perform incantations, you not only speak words but also embody what you are saying intensely and repeatedly. When you are saying positive things, you accompany the message with your entire body and add emphasis to your words. You use your hands, arms, facial expressions, and more, so you really believe what you are telling yourself with body, mind, and soul.

---

98 Toby Robbins, 2018.

IMRAN

Imran is in his early 20s, and as far back as he can remember, he has always been highly visual. His preferred learning tools were learning maps, graphs, and images, and he would spend hours rewriting his notes into a colorful, visually appealing form. When Imran developed anxiety, he turned to NLP techniques to minimize his stress triggers and boost his sense of well-being. His favorite exercise was the "Swish," which I will share with you below.

WHAT IS NEUROLINGUISTIC PROGRAMMING (NLP?)

Neuro-linguistic programming (NLP) is a coaching system devised in the 1970s by Richard Bandler, John Grinder, and Frank Pucelik. It has been used in a myriad of settings, including:

- helping people see life through a more positive lens
- improving relationships
- helping people achieve goals
- boosting self-awareness
- improving one's physical and mental wellbeing

Three studies undertaken in 2021 showed support for reducing pain post-surgery, promoting conscientiousness and job satisfaction, and fostering flexibility, motivation, positive mood, planning abilities, and better conflict resolution and problem-solving skills[99].

----

99 Raypole, 2022.

NEURO-LINGUISTIC PROGRAMMING

The creators explain the name of their methodology as follows[100]:

Neuro refers to the mental, emotional, and physical sides of your neurological system.

Linguistics refers to the language and communication patterns you employ when communicating with yourself or others.

Programming refers to how your emotions, thoughts, and behaviors can impact your current state of mind.

NLP METHODS

NLP practitioners use five main methods:

- **Affirmations** are simple statements that help you direct your focus away from your weaknesses and toward your strengths.
- **Hypnosis** is a changed state of awareness and heightened relaxation that boosts focus.
- **Reframing** means using evidence to help you change negative thoughts and emotions into positive ones.
- **Anchoring** is associating an internal response with an external or internal trigger so that the response can be quickly accessed when you need it.
- **Meditation** focuses on training in awareness and taking on a healthy perspective.

----

100 Raypole, 2022.

4 NLP EXERCISES TO HEAL YOUR INNER CHILD

It's now time to try out a few NLP exercises that can help you heal from the pain you have experienced in life.

Exercise 1: Swish

This exercise instructs your brain to replace something you don't want with something you do want. To perform this exercise[101]:

Identify your trigger, which is the catalyst for your anxiety or unease. For example, if you get nervous before public speaking, the trigger could be a specific sight, sound, or sensation.

Imagine an image associated with the trigger. For instance, you might visualize yourself standing on a stage, about to give a speech.

Now, choose an alternative image. Instead of seeing yourself nervous on stage, envision yourself delivering a flawless and captivating presentation. Create a mental picture that empowers you.

You now have two images to work with: the unwanted one and the desired one. Bring the unwanted image to the forefront of your mind's eye, making it prominent and vivid. Then, create the desired image, but make it small and faint, placing it in the bottom left-hand corner of your mind's eye.

Now, it's time for the big swap over. In one precise move, "switch" the positions of the images as you say the word

----
101 NLP Essential Guide, n.d.

"Swish!" The undesired image will become tiny and move to the left corner of your imagined scene, while the positive image will move to the center, becoming bold and vivid.

Exercise 2: Dissolving Bad Memories

This exercise helps you dissolve the memories that are causing your inner child pain[102].

Head to a quiet spot. Think of a memory that is harmful to your inner child, one that you find hard to get rid of. Think of that memory and envision everything you see, hear, smell, and taste in that memory. Make the colors in the memory vivid and ensure the images in your memory are large. Think about something you learned from this bad experience. Make the memory even bigger, brighter, and more vivid. Suddenly, let the memory explode, leaving behind nothing but a useful lesson.

Exercise 3: Change the Language

Psychologist, Robert Dilts, proposed that people could understand themselves better based on six logical levels, which indicate the different degrees to which they think, feel, know, or speak. Lower levels involve superficial or concrete thoughts, while higher levels encompass more abstract, profound, and meaningful thoughts.

Dilts espoused that you could tell what logical level someone was operating on by the language they employed to describe an issue or problem. People can become stuck on one level and

----
102 NLP-Techniques.ORG, n.d.

feel that the obstacle they are facing is insurmountable. However, if they move to a higher level, they can obtain a unique perspective on the issue and begin seeing more options and possible environmental solutions.

The logical levels are usually presented as a pyramid. They represent six levels of thinking: environment, behavior, capability or competence, beliefs, identity, and spirituality. These levels are hierarchical. When you find that you are stuck in a problem, you can get unstuck by changing the language to another level.

In Exercise 3, the aim is simply to ask yourself questions in each of the levels, so you can obtain greater clarity the next time you feel like you are getting nowhere with a situation or person. Let's say the problem is that your colleague gets annoyed with you when you need to ask them a question. You feel like you are walking on eggshells whenever you need something from them.

At the lowest level (Environment), ask yourself questions like, "Where am I?" "Where does this problem happen?" For instance, your answer might be: "This problem occurs when I am at work."

Next, jump to the Behavior level and ask yourself, "What am I doing?" Example: "I am approaching my colleague to ask them a question."

Next is the Capabilities level. The question might be, "What do I know how to do? What skills do I have?" You might answer, "I know how to tell my colleague that I sometimes need to approach them for work purposes. I have good communication skills, and I can do so in a gentle, empathetic way, so they can let me know their needs too. For instance, they might prefer me to call them first or email them before interrupting them at their desk."

The next level is Values and Beliefs. The questions are, "What is important to me? What do I expect from this situation?" The answer might be: "It is important for me to work well as a team with my colleagues. I expect to find a way to get the information I need from my colleague while trying my best to take their needs into account."

Next is the Identity level. "Who am I?" Example: "I am a person who works hard but also takes others' needs into account."

Finally, we get to the Spirit Level. We ask ourselves, "What is my purpose? What part of this is greater than me?" Your answer might be, "My purpose is to be a great nurse. Our entire team is greater than myself, and we can find ways to work synergetically."

Exercise 4: Matching and Mirroring

To build a stronger bond with someone in your personal or professional life, try matching and mirroring them. This can be particularly useful if you are arguing with them or discussing a tense topic. Try matching their posture, as well as the volume, pitch, and speed of their voice. Also, mirror their body language—the way their body is positioned, their gestures, eye movements, etc. Finally, try to use some of the words they have so they feel really comfortable being around you.

ACT: ACCEPTANCE AND COMMITMENT THERAPY (ACT)

Acceptance and commitment therapy is similar to CBT, but it focuses less on changing negative thoughts and beliefs and more on accepting them and letting them go. ACT is defined by Hayes et al. (2006) as "a third-level cognitive behavioral intervention aimed at enhancing our psychological flexibility.[103]"

The idea is that you don't have to put the energy into avoiding, denying, or fighting inner emotions. You can accept that life is hard and commit to making specific changes in your behavior so you can move forward in your life[104].

What Conditions Are ACT Currently Being Used to Treat?

ACT is currently being used successfully to treat:

- anxiety
- depression
- OCD
- psychosis
- eating disorders
- substance abuse disorders
- workplace stress
- chronic pain

----

103 Ackerman, 2017.
104 Psychology Today, n.d.

Many of these issues overlap with inner child trauma.

The Six Core Processes Involved in ACT

ACT comprises six processes[105]:

1. **Acceptance:** This means recognizing and being okay with negative thoughts, emotions, and experiences without trying to deny or change them. The idea is to open yourself to your fears while also focusing on the things you can control now.
2. **Cognitive Defusion:** This process involves separating yourself from your thoughts by noticing them and being more aware of how you think. The goal is to watch your thoughts instead of seeing the world through them[106].
3. **Being Present:** Keep your mind "in the here and now" instead of in the past or future.
4. **Self as Context:** This is the idea that you are not your thoughts and emotions. You are a separate person with the power to focus on the things that matter most in your life—like being a great partner or parent or engaging in lifelong learning.
5. **Values:** Keep your values in mind, so you can make decisions that align with them.
6. **Committed Action:** Commit to actions that can help you achieve your long-term goals.

----

105 Steinberg Behavior Solutions, n.d.
106 Cognitive Behavioral Therapy Los Angeles, 2022.

Key Barriers to Self-Acceptance

Before commencing your ACT activities and worksheets, it helps to know the key barriers to self-acceptance. Doing so can help you assess them, think about how they affect your life, and bring you closer to acceptance and healing. The main barriers to self-acceptance are:

- self-criticism
- judgment
- social comparison
- poor emotional regulation
- unrealistic expectations
- unprocessed trauma/having a hurt inner child
- being motivated by external instead of internal rewards
- beliefs of defectiveness
- being disconnected from your inner child
- poor coping styles
- fear of being vulnerable

Try to think of how each of these barriers is stopping you from connecting with others and achieving your personal goals.

5 ACT ACTIVITIES TO HEAL YOUR INNER CHILD

Triggers, Behaviors, and Rewards

This exercise helps you analyze that the behaviors you choose to obtain an immediate reward may not be the most ideal[107].

Fill in the following tables:

Triggers	Behaviors	Immediate Rewards
Example: Rude drivers on the road	Yelling, speeding, or cutting the rude drivers off	A sense that I have "taught them a lesson."

Clarifying Your Values

This exercise aims to help you identify your values, so you can take steps to align your behaviors with these values[108].

1. **Work/Education:** How do you want to be to the people you work with/your clients/your classmates, etc.? What type of relationships do you wish to build? What personal qualities would you like to strengthen?
2. **Relationships:** How do you want to be in your relationships? What personal qualities do you want to develop?
3. **Personal Growth/Health and Wellbeing:** What steps are you taking to grow as a human being? What qualities would you like to develop?

----
107 Ackerman 2017.
108 Ackerman, 2017.

4. **Leisure:** How do you want to spend your free time? What personal qualities would you like to develop through them?

Now go through these answers and rate, from 1 to 10 (with 10 being the best outcome and 1 the worst), the extent to which you live according to your values in each of these three areas.

✎...

✎...

✎...

✎...

What Am I Repressing?

This exercise helps you think of the unpleasant thoughts or feelings you try to repress, often with negative results[109].

- The thoughts I'd most like to repress are___.
- The emotions I'd most like to repress are___.
- The sensations I'd most like to repress are___.
- The memories I'd most like to repress are___.

For each of the above, write down the strategies you used to repress them. These can include:

- distraction
- avoiding situations or opportunities
- worrying

---

109 Harris, 2008.

- keeping your mind in the past
- fantasizing about the future
- imagining that you are escaping from the things that cause you strife
- imagining revenge
- thinking how unfair it all is
- blaming others or the world
- talking positively to yourself
- using logic to talk to yourself
- trying to work yourself out
- trying to work out a situation
- trying to understand why others have done or said things
- any substances you may have used to make yourself feel better

✎...

✎...

✎...

✎...

Next, go through your list of strategies and ask yourself if they effectively ended your hurt in the long term. Ask yourself if they helped your life have more meaning.

If they did not help you, what did they cost you in terms of happiness, health, financial well-being, relationships, or energy?

Setting SMART Goals

This exercise aims to help you set realistic, achievable goals, not those which are too difficult to achieve. Setting achievable goals can help you live in tune with your values while also keeping you motivated[110].

Choose a goal that is:

1. **Specific:** The goal should be clearly defined. For instance, instead of saying, "I'll work harder," you might state, "My goal is to finish my next project two days early, so I have time to check it well."
2. **Measurable:** You should be able to measure if the goal has been achieved or not. In the above example, it is easy to tell if you managed to get your work done by the deadline.
3. **Achievable:** Your goal should be realistic. An example of an unrealistic goal is: "I'm going to lose 10 pounds in a week." A more realistic goal might be: "I'm going to lose 2 pounds in a week."
4. **Relevant:** Your goals should be worthwhile, pertinent to you, and timely. It should be applicable to your current socio-economic environment, too.

For example, you might want to learn a new language, but you are particularly busy at work because you have a big project that will take two months to complete. You may not have time right now to learn a new language and give it your all. It might

---

110 Boogard, 2021.

be a more applicable goal in two months' time when your project is done.

5. **Time-Bound:** Give yourself a reasonable time frame to complete your goal, but try to have a general time frame for achieving it. You can break your goal into smaller chunks and set individual deadlines for each smaller goal[111].

✎...

✎...

✎...

✎...

You have honed NLP and ACT skills, in addition to making CBT part of your daily life. We hope that these exercises have all done their share to make your inner child feel stronger, happier, and better equipped to tackle all life's challenges with courage and love.

----

111 Mind Tools, n.d.

INVITE OTHER READERS TO MEET
THE MOST IMPORTANT PERSON THEY
ARE LIKELY TO MEET IN THEIR
LIFETIME—THEIR INNER CHILD.

You now know how you can embrace a healthy attachment style, and you have so many tools to reframe your thoughts and core beliefs into positive, empowering ones. You know that emotional intelligence is even more important than your IQ, and you have also harnessed the power of incantations, NLP, and ACT.

Simply by sharing your honest opinion of this book on Amazon, you'll show others where they can find the guidance they need. You will inspire them to meet their inner child, heal them through love and acceptance, and give in to childlike playfulness when life gets too serious.

WANT TO HELP OTHERS?

Thank you so much for your support. I wish you and your inner child a close, loving relationship now and in years to come.

CONCLUSION

"One of the most courageous decisions you'll ever make is to finally let go of what is hurting your heart and soul."

— BRIGITTE NICOLE

In this book, you have met, conversed with, and taken steps to heal your inner child. Hopefully, you have made many discoveries along the way … from needs that have not been met in your childhood to the negative filters or cognitive distortions that are stopping you from making positive progress.

Despite the fact that this may be the first time you have acknowledged your inner child, they have always been there, inside of you, ready to come out to express their unmet needs, have a "tantrum," and sometimes, simply play. Your inner child, in many ways, represents the most painful but also the most joyful aspects of your personality, values, and identity, and cherishing their existence is the first step toward healing.

In this book, we have taken many steps toward understanding the link between your hurt inner child and obstacles that may be standing in the way of your happiness and well-being. We have seen, for instance, how trauma encountered in childhood impacts your attachment style and how you interact with others.

The hurt you experienced in your early years can also harm your self-esteem by instilling false beliefs in your heart about your own lack of worth. Throughout the book, we have highlighted the powerful effect that cognitive behavioral therapy can have on countering negative thoughts and beliefs. By getting rid of harmful cognitive distortions and using available evidence to get a clearer picture of things, you can stop being your own worst enemy and get rid of self-sabotaging behaviors. We have also suggested CBT as a powerful way to experiment with new behaviors so that your thoughts and beliefs can, in turn, be positively impacted.

We also highlighted the value of building your emotional intelligence. A hurt inner child can sometimes manifest through the unregulated expression of powerful emotions like anger, sadness, or fear. By building your emotional awareness and understanding and working on reasoning with and managing your emotions, you can use these emotions to effect positive change. Emotions like anger send you a loud and clear signal that your boundaries are not being respected. You can choose to respond to this signal through healthy means—for instance, by assertively stating your boundaries and refusing to allow others to disrespect them.

Strengthening your emotional intelligence will also help you deal with disappointment, pain, and stress more productively. While you certainly cannot avoid these challenges in your daily life, you can employ powerful strategies such as accepting negative feedback, taking accountability for your actions, and moving on after making mistakes. By adopting a growth mindset, you can see failure as a unique opportunity to switch up your approach and strategize for better outcomes from challenging situations.

We provided you with a host of CBT exercises that will help you to acknowledge your inner child, find out what they need, and start taking steps toward healing. We have also explored other methods being embraced in inner child therapy—including neuro-linguistic programming and acceptance and commitment therapy (ACT). NLP has a host of useful exercises (including the Swish exercise) which help you minimize your fears and maximize your courage. ACT, meanwhile, is firmly focused on accepting challenging thoughts and beliefs and then moving beyond them.

You are so much more than your thoughts and beliefs. Your inner child may rant and rave, but in the end, they are simply trying to tell you that your voice deserves to be heard and your wants and needs deserve to be met. You and only you can take steps to heal the pain caused by others.

Your inner child possesses invaluable information about the things that cause you the most pain. Rather than burying or suppressing them, invite them to talk to you, listen to them with an open heart, and take the steps you need to move beyond the pain to a beautiful, non-judgmental, accepting state of childlikeness.

Don't forget to tap into the most joyful side of your inner child, too. In addition to journaling, asking yourself questions, and trying to find the answers within, take time to do the things you love, laugh with reckless abandon, and pursue the activities that made you happiest when life was an adventure filled with wonder.

THANKS FOR READING MY BOOK!

I genuinely trust that you found this book enjoyable and that the insights shared within it will be of value to you.

I would greatly appreciate it if you could spare a moment to share your honest thoughts in the form of a review or star rating on Amazon. (Providing a star rating is a quick and simple process).

Your review serves as a helpful resource for fellow young adults seeking this book, potentially guiding them on their own life journeys. Plus, it's a wonderful way to spread positive karma your way.

Scan this code to leave a review.

NOTES

INTRODUCTION

1. Wisner, 2022.

1. WHO IS YOUR INNER CHILD?

1. Downey & Crummy, 2022.
2. Trieu, 2023.
3. Davis, 2020.
4. Assagioli, 1973.
5. Rediscovering Sacredness, n.d.
6. LePera, 2021.
7. Wisteria Edwards, 2021.
8. Gatt, n.d.
9. Health Vista, n.d.
10. Cherry, 2023.
11. McLeod, 2018.
12. Raypole, 2020.
13. Williams, 2022.

2. HOW YOUR CHILDHOOD EXPERIENCES INFLUENCE YOUR ATTACHMENT STYLE

1. Cherry, 2023.
2. Mandriota, 2021.
3. Edward, 2017.
4. Ryder, 2022.
5. Newport Academy, 2017.
6. Firestone, n.d.
7. Sutton, 2022.
8. Sutton, n.d.

9. Callisto Media Books, n.d.

3. WHAT IS CBT AND HOW CAN IT HELP YOU HEAL YOUR INNER CHILD?

1. Pun, 2019.
2. Hasanović et al., 2006.
3. American Psychological Association, n.d.
4. Bennett, 2018.
5. Bennett, 2018.
6. Content Works, 2022.
7. Robinson & Smith, n.d.
8. Shatz, n.d.
9. The University of Kansas, n.d.
10. Single Care, 2023.
11. Kekatos, 2023.
12. Wooll, 2021.
13. Calechman, 2022.
14. McLeod, 2023.
15. Psycholotron, n.d.
16. Therapist Aid, n.d.
17. Compitus, 2020.

4. STEP 1: REFRAME THE THOUGHTS THAT HURT YOUR INNER CHILD

1. Robinson, n.d.
2. Arocho, 2022.
3. Kiken & Shook, 2014.
4. Mindful, n.d.
5. Positive Psychology, n.d.
6. Brenner et al., 2020.
7. Introsport, 2018.
8. Cronkleton, 2023.
9. Gratitude Blog, n.d.
10. Health Direct, n.d.

11. Pangilinan, 2022.

5. STEP 2: REFRAME THE BELIEFS THAT HURT YOUR INNER CHILD

1. The Relationship Guy, n.d.
2. Science Daily, 2007.
3. Robinson & Smith, n.d.
4. Braden et al., 2009.
5. Marobella, 2023.
6. Scott, 2022.
7. Help Guide, n.d.
8. Help Guide, n.d.
9. Griggs, 2020.
10. Therapist Aid, n.d.
11. Schaffner, 2020.
12. Therapist Aid, n.d.

6. STEP 3: EXPERIMENT WITH NEW BEHAVIORS

1. Brown, 2020.
2. Anne Silvers, n.d.
3. Brennan, 2021.
4. Lifestyle Desk, 2019.
5. Riverside Recovery, 2019.
6. Taylor, 2021.
7. Scott, 2022.
8. James Madison University, n.d.
9. Wooll, 2022.
10. Weinstock, 2023.
11. Brooten-Brooks, 2022.
12. Mental Health America, n.d.
13. Wooll, 2022.
14. Morin, 2020.
15. Washington University, n.d.

7. STEP 4: BUILD YOUR EMOTIONAL INTELLIGENCE

1. Cornerstone University, 2017.
2. Cherry, 2023.
3. Harvard Professional Development, n.d.
4. Custom Insight, n.d.
5. Firstup, n.d.
6. Therapist Aid, n.d.
7. Lavelda Naylor, n.d.

8. STEP 5: OVERCOME YOUR INNER CHILD'S ENEMIES

1. Cherry, 2022.
2. Laguardia & Michalsen, 2017.
3. Hyland, 2022.
4. Wright, 2021.
5. Department of Educational Psychology SNDT Women's University, n.d.
6. Online Learning College, 2022.
7. Cherry, 2022.
8. Raypole, 2021.
9. Ackerman, 2018.
10. Ackerman, 2018.
11. Utah Education Network, n.d.
12. Virginia Counseling, n.d.

9. BONUS CHAPTER: NLP AND ACT FOR INNER CHILD HEALING

1. Toby Robbins, 2018.
2. Raypole, 2022.
3. Raypole, 2022.
4. NLP Essential Guide, n.d.
5. NLP-Techniques.ORG, n.d.
6. Ackerman, 2017.

7. Psychology Today, n.d.
8. Steinberg Behavior Solutions, n.d.
9. Cognitive Behavioral Therapy Los Angeles, 2022.
10. Ackerman 2017.
11. Ackerman, 2017.
12. Harris, 2008.
13. Boogard, 2021.
14. Mind Tools, n.d.

REFERENCES

Ackerman, C. E. (2017, March 1). *How does acceptance and commitment therapy (ACT) work?* Positive Psychology. https://positivepsychology.com/act-acceptance-and-commitment-therapy/#act-worksheets

Ackerman, C. (2018, June 7). *What is self-concept theory? A psychologist explains.* Positive Psychology. https://positivepsychology.com/self-concept/#examples-self-concept

American Psychological Association. (n.d.). *What is cognitive behavioral therapy?* https://www.apa.org/ptsd-guideline/patients-and-families/cognitive-behavioral

Anne Silvers. (n.d.). *Brené Brown vulnerability definition and quotes with images.* https://annsilvers.com/blogs/news/brene-brown-vulnerability-definition-and-quotes

Arocho, J. (2022, December 5). *All-or-nothing thinking: Examples and how it causes depression and anxiety.* Manhattan Center for Cognitive Behavioral Therapy. https://www.manhattancbt.com/all-or-nothing-thinking/

Assagioli, R. (1973). *The Conflict between the Generations and the Psychosynthesis of the Human Ages* (Vol. 31). New York: Psychosynthesis Research Foundation.

Bennett, T. (2018, January 12). *6 everyday behaviors that negatively affect your mental health.* Thriveworks. https://thriveworks.com/blog/everyday-behaviors-negatively-affect-mental-health/

Boogard, K. (2021, December 26). *How to write SMART goals.* Atlassian. https://www.atlassian.com/blog/productivity/how-to-write-smart-goals#:

Braden, R., Reichow, S., & Halm, M. A. (2009, December). The use of the essential oil lavandin to reduce preoperative anxiety in surgical patients. *Journal of Perianesthesia Nursing, 24*(6), 348-355. https://doi.org/10.1016/j.jopan.2009.10.002

Brennan, D. (2021, August 17). *Perfectionism: 6 consequences to watch out for.* WebMD. https://www.webmd.com/balance/features/consequences-perfectionism#:

Brenner, J., LeBlang, S. D., Lizotte-Waniewski, M., Schmidt, B., Espinosa, P. S., DeMets, D. L., Newberg, A. B., & Hennekens, C. H. (2020). Mindfulness with paced breathing reduces blood pressure. *Medical Hypotheses, 142*, 109780. https://doi.org/10.1016/j.mehy.2020.109780

Brooten-Brooks, M. C. (2022, January 24). *What is boundary setting?* Verywell Health. https://www.verywellhealth.com/setting-boundaries-5208802

Brown, B. (2020, October 3). *The power of vulnerability.* [Video]. https://www.ted.com/talks/brene_brown_the_power_of_vulnerability/c/transcript

Calechman, S. (2022, May 2). *How to break a bad habit.* Harvard Health Publishing. https://www.health.harvard.edu/blog/how-to-break-a-bad-habit-202205022736

Callisto Media Books. (n.d.). *Attachment theory worksheets.* https://callistomediabooks.com/AttachmentTheory/Worksheets_Attachment_Theory_Workbook.pdf

Cherry, K. (2022, November 7). *What is self-concept?* Verywell Mind. https://www.verywellmind.com/what-is-self-concept-2795865

Cherry, K. (2022, November 7). *What is the fight-or-flight response?* VeryWell Mind. https://www.verywellmind.com/what-is-the-fight-or-flight-response-2795194

Cherry, K. (2023, February 22). *What is attachment theory? The importance of early emotional bonds.* Verywell Mind. https://www.verywellmind.com/what-is-attachment-theory-2795337

Cherry, K. (2023, March 14). *Biography of Abraham Maslow (1908-1970).* Verywell Mind. https://www.verywellmind.com/biography-of-abraham-maslow-1908-1970-2795524#:

Cherry, K. (2023, May 2). *Emotional intelligence: How we perceive, evaluate, express, and control emotions.* Verywell Mind. https://www.verywellmind.com/what-is-emotional-intelligence-2795423

Cognitive Behavioral Therapy Los Angeles. (2022, August 9). *Cognitive defusion techniques and exercises.* https://cogbtherapy.com/cbt-blog/cognitive-defusion-techniques-and-exercises

Compitus, K. (2020, September 12). *What is a functional analysis of behavior in CBT?* Positive Psychology. https://positivepsychology.com/functional-analysis-cbt/#perform

Content Works. (2022, July 12). *Social media in the USA – The stats you need to know.* https://contentworks.agency/social-media-in-the-usa-the-stats-you-need-to-know/

Cornerstone University. (2017, June 5). *Are you emotionally intelligent? Here's how to tell.* https://www.cornerstone.edu/blog-post/are-you-emotionally-intelligent-heres-how-to-tell/

Cronkleton, A. (2023, March 24). *10 breathing techniques for stress relief and more.* Healthline. https://www.healthline.com/health/breathing-exercise

Custom Insight. (n.d.). *What is 360 degree feedback?* https://www.custominsight.com/360-degree-feedback/what-is-360-degree-feedback.asp#:

Davis, S. (2020, July 13). *The wounded inner child.* CPTSD Foundation. https://cptsdfoundation.org/2020/07/13/the-wounded-inner-child/#:

Department of Educational Psychology SNDT Women's University. (n.d.). *Aspects and components of self concept continued.* http://detsndt.ac.in/nmeict-files/nmeict-los/edupsycho/ep8/8.1.2/

Downey, C., & Crummy, A. (2022, February). The impact of childhood trauma on children's wellbeing and adult behavior. *European Journal of Trauma & Dissociation, 6*(1). https://doi.org/10.1016/j.ejtd.2021.100237

Edward, D. (2017, April 8). *Schaffer & Emerson's four stages of attachment.* Psychology Unlocked. https://www.psychologyunlocked.com/schaffer-emerson/

Firestone, L. (n.d.). *How your attachment style affects your parenting.* PsychAlive. https://www.psychalive.org/how-your-attachment-style-affects-your-parenting/#:

Firstup. (n.d.). *15 ways to improve diversity and inclusion in the workplace.* https://firstup.io/blog/15-ways-to-improve-diversity-and-inclusion-in-the-workplace/

Gatt, R. (n.d.). *4 benefits of inner child work.* Woven Together. https://woventraumatherapy.com/blog/4-benefits-of-inner-child-work

Gratitude Blog. (n.d.). *111 self-care affirmations for inner child, peace, and gratitude.* https://blog.gratefulness.me/self-care-affirmations/

Griggs, U. (2020, November 27). *How to overcome your resistance to change for a better self.* Life Hack. https://www.lifehack.org/822909/resistance-to-change

Harris, R. (2008). *Worksheets to use with the happiness trap.* The Happiness Trap. https://thehappinesstrap.com/upimages/The_Complete_Happiness_Trap_Worksheets.pdf.pdf

Harvard Professional Development. (n.d.). *How to improve your emotional intelligence.* https://professional.dce.harvard.edu/blog/how-to-improve-your-emotional-intelligence/

Hasanović, M., Sinanović, O., Selimbasić, Z., Pajević, I.,& Avdibegović, E. (2006, February). Psychological disturbances of war-traumatized children from different foster and family settings in Bosnia and Herzegovina. *Croatian Medical Journal, 47*(1), 85–94. https://www.ncbi.nlm.nih.gov/pmc/articles/PMC2080380/

Health Direct. (n.d.). *Self-talk.* https://www.healthdirect.gov.au/self-talk

Health Vista. (n.d.). *Healing your inner child.* https://healthvista.net/wp-content/uploads/2015/05/HealingYourInnerChildHandout.pdf

Help Guide. (n.d.). *Stress management: How to reduce and relive stress.* https://www.helpguide.org/articles/stress/stress-management.htm

Hyland, S. (2022, May 10). *What are the three stages of fight-or-flight? The 3 stages of stress response explained.* A. Vogel. https://www.avogel.co.uk/health/stress-anxiety-low-mood/stress/what-are-the-three-stages-of-fight-or-flight/

Introsport. (2018, July 30). *Alternate nostril breathing– Yoga technique.* [Video]. YouTube. https://youtu.be/G8xIEzX40bA

James Madison University. (n.d.). *Counseling center: People pleasing.* https://www.jmu.edu/counselingctr/self-help/relationships/people-pleasing.shtml#:

Kassim, D. (2022, October 23). *A guide to using essential oil for skin. Purodem.* https://www.purodem.com/guide-to-using-essential-oil-for-skin/

Kekatos, M. (2023, January 26). *Only about half of US adults are meeting physical activity guidelines: CDC.* https://abcnews.go.com/Health/half-us-adults-meeting-physical-activity-guidelines-cdc/story?id=96689335#:

Kiken, L.G., & Shook, N.J. (2014, December). Does mindfulness attenuate thoughts emphasizing negativity, but not positivity? *Journal of Research in Personality, 53*, 22-30. https://doi.org/10.1016/j.jrp.2014.08.002

Laguardia, F., & Michalsen, V. (2017). Trigger warnings: From panic to data. Montclair State University. https://digitalcommons.montclair.edu/cgi/viewcontent.cgi?article=1032&context=justice-studies-facpubs

Lavenda Naylor. (n.d.). *Need to better understand yourself? Try the personal iceberg.* https://laveldanaylor.wordpress.com/2012/10/09/need-to-stop-doing-something-try-the-personal-iceberg/

LePera, N. (2021). *How to do the work: recognize your patterns, heal from your past, and create your self.* First edition. New York, NY, Harper Wave, an imprint of HarperCollinsPublishers.

Lifestyle Desk. (2019, October 28). *Image is powerful but also superficial: Cameron Russell.* Indian Express. https://indianexpress.com/article/life style/life-positive/image-is-powerful-body-positivity-inspirational-quotes-6088054/

Mandriota, M. (2021, October 13). *Here is how to identify your attachment style.* PsychCentral. https://psychcentral.com/health/4-attachment-styles-in-relationships

Marobella, P. (2023, February 13). *The importance of creativity: The positive effect on your brain and health.* LinkedIn. https://www.linkedin.com/pulse/impor tance-creativity-positive-effect-your-brain-health-marobella/

McLeod, S. (2018, May 21). *Maslow's Hierarchy of Needs.* Simply Psychology. https://canadacollege.edu/dreamers/docs/Maslows-Hierarchy-of-Needs.pdf

McLeod, S. (2023, May 10). *Stanford prison experiment: Zimbardo's famous study.* Simply Psychology. https://www.simplypsychology.org/zimbardo.html

Mental Health America. (n.d.). *Helpful vs harmful: Ways to manage emotions.* https://www.mhanational.org/helpful-vs-harmful-ways-manage-emotions

Mind Tools. (n.d.). *SMART goals.* https://www.mindtools.com/a4wo118/smart-goals

Mindful. (n.d.). *Getting started with mindfulness.* https://www.mindful.org/meditation/mindfulness-getting-started/

Morales-Brown, L. (2020, October 30). *Attachment disorder in adults: What is it?* Medical New Today. https://www.medicalnewstoday.com/articles/attach ment-disorder-in-adults

Morin, A. (2020, February 12). *How to perform behavioral experiments.* Verywell Mind. https://www.verywellmind.com/how-to-perform-behavioral-experiments-4779864#:

Newport Academy. *How relational trauma impacts teen mental health, social connections, and self-esteem.* https://www.newportacademy.com/resources/mental-health/relational-trauma/#:

NLP Essential Guide. (n.d.). 2-7 swish examples: Size, brightness, distance. https://nlpessentialguide.com/nlp-swish-pattern/

NLP-Techniques.ORG. (n.d.). *NLP technique: Exploding bad memories.* https://www.nlp-techniques.org/what-is-nlp/nlp-technique-exploding-bad-memories/

Online Learning College. (2022, May 31). *Carl Rogers.* https://online-learn ing-college.com/knowledge-hub/gcses/gcse-psychology-help/carl-rogers/

Pangilinan, J. (2022, November 16). *8 printable negative self-talk worksheets for 2023.* Happier Human. https://www.happierhuman.com/negative-self-talk-worksheets/

Positive Psychology, n.d. *Breath Awareness.* https://positive.b-cdn.net/wp-content/uploads/Breath-Awareness.pdf

Psychology Today. (n.d.). *Acceptance and commitment therapy.* https://www.psychologytoday.com/us/therapy-types/acceptance-and-commitment-therapy

Psycholotron. (n.d.). *Functions of attitudes.* http://psychlotron.org.uk/ resources/social/AS_AQB_social_attitudes_function.pdf

Pun, J. (2019, October 22). *What is online cognitive-behavorial therapyt (CBT)?* Starling Minds. https://www.starlingminds.com/what-is-online-cogni tive-behavioral-therapy-cbt-starling-minds/#:

Raypole, C. (2020, February 27). *A (realistic) guide to becoming self-actualized.* Healthline. https://www.healthline.com/health/self-actualization

Raypole, C. (2021, February 5). *Breaking down the habit loop.* Healthline. https://www.healthline.com/health/mental-health/habit-loop

Raypole, C. (2022, June 14). *Can neurolinguistic programming really transform your life?* Healthline. https://www.healthline.com/health/nlp-therapy

Rediscovering Sacredness. (n.d.). *Inner-child healing work: Your inner child says "Wake up!"* https://rediscoveringsacredness.com/inner-child-healing-work-your-inner-child-wants-you-to-wake-up/

Riverside Recovery. (2019, June 17). *Why do we self-blame?* https://rrtampa. com/do-we-self-blame/#:

Robinson, G. (n.d.). *The enemy within: Are your thoughts sabotaging your success?* Attorney at Work. https://www.attorneyatwork.com/the-enemy-within-be-aware-of-your-inner-thoughts/

Robinson, L., & Smith, M. (n.d.). *The role social media plays in mental health.* Help Guide. https://www.helpguide.org/articles/mental-health/social-media-and-mental-health.htm#:

Robinson, M., & Smith, M. (n.d.). *Stress management: How to reduce and relieve stress.* Help Guide. https://www.helpguide.org/articles/stress/stress-management.htm

Ryder, G. (2022, January 19). *What is attachment trauma?* PsychCentral. https://psychcentral.com/health/attachment-trauma

Schaffner, A. K. (2o2o, June 26). *Core beliefs: 12 worksheets to challenge negative beliefs.* Positive Psychology. https://positivepsychology.com/core-beliefs-worksheets/

Science Daily. (2007, May 16). *Treating oneself kindly when things go badly could be a key to weathering life's challenges, researchers say.* https://www.sciencedaily.com/releases/2007/05/070516081014.htm

Scott, E. (2022, October 19). *18 effective stress relief strategies.* VeryWell Mind. https://www.verywellmind.com/tips-to-reduce-stress-3145195

Scott, E. (2022, October 31). *Avoidance coping and why it creates additional stress.* VeryWell Mind. https://www.verywellmind.com/avoidance-coping-and-stress-4137836#:

Shatz, I. (n.d.). *Procrastination statistics: Interesting and useful statistics about procrastination.* Solving Procrastination. https://solvingprocrastination.com/procrastination-statistics/#:

Single Care. (2023, February 3). *Sleep statistics 2023.* https://www.singlecare.com/blog/news/sleep-statistics/#:

Steinberg Behavior Solutions. (n.d.). *Applying the six core ACT processes during the current pandemic crisis.* https://www.sbsaba.com/applying-the-six-core-act-processes-during-the-current-pandemic-crisis/#:

Sutton, J. (2022, June 30). *Attachment style in therapy: 6 worksheets & handouts.* Positive Psychology. https://positivepsychology.com/attachment-style-worksheets/#discovering

Sutton, J. (n.d.). *Accepting yourself as being perfectly imperfect.* Positive Psychology. https://positive.b-cdn.net/wp-content/uploads/2022/03/Accepting-Yourself-As-Being-Perfectly-Imperfect.pdf

Taylor, M. (2021, August 17). *Perfectionism: 6 consequences to watch for.* WebMD. https://www.webmd.com/balance/features/consequences-perfectionism#:

The Relationship Guy. (n.d.). *The real reason you're unhappy: Your inner rules.* https://therelationshipguy.com/the-real-reason-you-are-unhappy-your-inner-rules-7452377142/

The University Kansas. (n.d.). *Procrastination.* https://caps.ku.edu/procrastination#:

Therapist Aid. (n.d.). *Challenging questions worksheet.* https://positive.b-cdn.net/wp-content/uploads/Disputing-Irrational-Beliefs.pdf

Therapist Aid. (n.d.). *Core beliefs.* https://www.therapistaid.com/worksheets/core-beliefs

Therapist Aid. (n.d.). *Emotional regulation skills.* https://www.therapistaid.com/worksheets/dbt-emotion-regulation-skills

Therapist Aid. (n.d.). *Fact or opinion.* https://www.therapistaid.com/worksheets/fact-or-opinion

Tiny Buddha. (n.d.). *The quote archive.* https://tinybuddha.com/wisdom-quotes/our-brains-are-wired-for-connection/

Tony Robbins. (2018). *The power of incantations.* [Video]. YouTube. https://youtu.be/rzT73D15TKk

Trieu, T. (2023, April 10). *What is inner child work? A guide to healing your inner child.* Mind Body Green. https://www.mindbodygreen.com/articles/inner-child-work

Utah Education Network. (n.d.). *Self concept.* https://www.uen.org/lessonplan/view/29132

Virginia Counseling. (n.d.). *(Free) classical conditioning worksheets to break bad habits.* https://www.vacounseling.com/classical-conditioning-worksheet/

Washington University. (n.d.). *Doing exposure worksheet.* https://depts.washington.edu/uwhatc/PDF/TF-%20CBT/pages/5%20CBT%20for%20Anxiety/Doing%20Exposure%20Worksheet.pdf

Weinstock, C. P. (2023, January 4). *All about boundary setting: Why do it and how to get better at it.* Everyday Health. https://www.everydayhealth.com/emotional-health/all-about-boundary-setting-why-do-it-and-how-to-get-better-at-it/#:

Williams, P. (2022, November 18). *Your wounded inner child is affecting your adult relationships.* Medium. https://medium.com/the-conscious-way/your-wounded-inner-child-is-affecting-your-adult-relationships-76b3c95f19e2

Wisner, W. (2022, February 24). *What Are Adverse Childhood Experiences (ACEs)?* Verywell Mind. https://www.verywellmind.com/what-are-aces-adverse-childhood-experiences-5219030

Wooll, M. (2021, July 26). *A growth mindset is a must-have — these 13 tips will grow yours.* BetterUp. https://www.betterup.com/blog/growth-mindset

Wooll, M. (2022, February 12). *How to challenge yourself to start living your best life every day.* BetterUp. https://www.betterup.com/blog/how-to-challenge-yourself

Wooll, M. (2022, February 9). *Overworked? Signs to spot if it's a problem.* BetterUp. https://www.betterup.com/blog/working-too-much#:

Wright, S. (2021, November 8). *How to identify and overcome trauma triggers.* PsychCentral. https://psychcentral.com/health/trauma-triggers

Wysteria Edwards. (n.d.). *7 inner child archetypes.* https://www.wysteriaedwards.com/blog/7%20Inner%20Child%20Archetypes

Printed in Great Britain
by Amazon

50064896R00118